Hymns From The Temple
A Hellenic Book of Prayer

Lykeia

Hymns From The Temple

A Hellenic Book of Prayer

Lykeia

Asphodel Press

Hubbardston, Massachusetts

Asphodel Press
12 Simond Hill Road
Hubbardston, MA 01452

Hymns from the Temple: A Hellenic Book of Prayer
© 2010 Lykeia
ISBN 978-0-9825798-1-7

All rights reserved.
No part of this book may be reproduced in any form
or by any means without the permission of the author.

Printed in cooperation with
Lulu Enterprises, Inc.
860 Aviation Parkway, Suite 300
Morrisville, NC 27560

This volume is dedicated to Apollon and the Nine Muses who never cease in their divine inspiration; I gave thanks and offerings to you for the words whispered to my ear on the wind. For my daughter and husband, my wonderful family who surround me in unconditional love. And lastly a big thank you to you, the reader.

Contents

I The Olympians
- Hestia 3
- Ares 7
- Artemis 10
- Hephaistos 20
- Hera 23
- Poseidon 28
- Athena 33
- Aphrodite 37
- Apollon 40
- Hermes 57
- Zeus 63
- Demeter 70

II The Daughter And The Son
- Persephone 81
- Dionysos 88

III The Titans And Primordial Gods
- Nyx 97
- Ge/Gaia 101
- Kronos 102
- Tethys 104
- Eros 106
- Helios 110
- Selene 115
- Prometheus 119
- Leto 121
- Hekate 124

IV Other Gods
- Pan 130
- Hades 133
- Hypnos 135
- Iris 136

Muses 138
Nymphs 142
Hyacinthos.. 150
Ariadne 152
Adonis 154
Semele 157
Orpheus 159
About the Author *162*

I
The Olympians

The twelve most high gods, known as the Olympians, are perhaps the most well-known and beloved gods worldwide. As children we grow up hearing the myths of their reign, their sacred rites, their loves, and the pursuits of their children. They are not long-ago half-forgotten deities, obscured in the mists of history. They are worshipped and loved. They are here all around us, impacting our lives. The first section of this book contains prayers and hymns to the Olympians: Zeus, Hera, Ares, Aphrodite, Artemis, Apollon, Hestia, Hephaistos, Hermes, Athena, Poseidon, and Demeter. The gods have a multitude of festivals that these hymns can be incorporated into, or can be used in daily devotional activities. For more information about the gods I highly recommend http://www.theoi.com, the works of Aeschylus and Euripedes, and the Homeric and Orphic Hymns.

Hestia

Hestia is the first-born child of Rhea and Kronos, and as such she is the first we honor in our prayers and rituals. She is the goddess of the hearth and sacrificial fire, dwelling in homes both mortal and divine. Hestia is present in every living flame, an eternal virgin who is beloved by all but belongs to none. We honor her in the warmth of our homes and families, as the goddess who tends the house of Apollon, and the hearth-keeper of Olympos. The mule of the grain mills is sacred to her.

Hestia
First-born, flame-born, fire-dwelling goddess,
Goddess of creation, as the glacial ice releases its hold,
And the water rushes, ever flowing to the sea.
The trickling drops flow into the cavern, as ore to the mold
And by this power the sweet spring up-wells
To bring life to the engraved sweep of earth.
You are the free-moving fire, the first spark in night,
The yawning volcanic mouth, a crack in the shell's ornate girth
Drawing up the rich minerals to bear forth the trembling shoot.
Round and round life turns, but always returns to you
The seasons churn, spring blossom yields to autumn wheat;
The spans of ice reach and go, volcanoes sleep and spew.
Ever changing, ever evolving, this is your throne,
Mother of Life, magmatic empress, queen of the home.

To Hestia
Sing to the high-sparking altar flames, and to burning hearth fires,
That there at the side of that flaming light Hestia sits tending.
The warm flame bathes her face, her delicate arm and hand,
Into her consuming embrace all offerings are to the gods received,
For there she lurks in every place, offerings poured, where fire stirs.
Hail Hestia first and last, your light begins it all and its embers end,

Ever are you dear friend to immortal gods and the families of man.
As the burning flame spans distance, everywhere at one time,
So you dwell in every place, great house of Zeus and mortal space.
Beloved fiery one, by your hand offerings burn and the oven bakes,
Demeter provides the ground grain, but the bread is your gift by flame.
Light flickers, a necessity for men, and so your oil feeds the torch,
You drip of oil, fragrant Hestia, it flows from your combed curls,
The sweet-scented drops feed the ever-hungry consuming sparks.
Sweet familial hearth, kindly goddess, to who all gather and adore,
Sheltering arms embrace the families close around her eternal light,
Feasting, well-fed, protected from the elements that nature rages.
Domestic-loving goddess, sweet-faced maiden without guile or deceit,
Calm, slow-dancing, deftly weaving together the ties of familial bonds!
Hail Hestia, mother of many, never have birthed, and never have loved,
Your warm and pure heart extends in love and compassion to all.

Fire of Hestia

Hail to Hestia, first and last to all,
Where the burning fire lights, or extinguished dark,
But when the earthly light is dark in the winter months,
It burns so bright in its hidden place underneath the earth.
Hail to you goddess of the altar, of the flame, of the hearth.

One there you rest deep within,
One with the earth, within the flesh,
Seated and enthroned in the deepest place,
Kindled on the sacred altars that forever burn.

In your flame the bread is baked that nourishes all,
To nourish the body to nourish the mortal soul,
Divine provider and nurturer of millions of the earth.
There too burns the incense, the laurel, rise to sweet perfume,
A twisting rise of smoke rising to mingle with the ether,
To delight all hearts among men and highest gods.

Bringer of vitality, you wear the orange-bright headdress,
And your fingers drip with fragrant oil where the fire blooms,
Shining reflection in the liquid molten gold of your immortal eyes,
Flushed upon the rosy glow of your cheek and soft lip.

Without you life would be dust, to lay in forever sleep,
Barren life, all the gods would have closed their eyes.
Ares would not move to strike, where would be Apollo's luster glow?
And there would be Demeter dully gowned, her eyes withdrawn,
No passion would stir; Eros would not unite lovers on Aphrodite's bed,
And then fade away, dust scattered to the wind, the mortal races end.

So hail to bright-browed Hestia who bears the blooming tree.

Hymn to Hestia

Goddess of the red lace veil, sitting by the fireside,
Maiden of the kindling box, first spark of light,
Hearth-tender dwelling within the heart of all things,
Hestia, bloom-cheeked goddess, child who breaks the night.
Holy daughter of Kronos, Hestia the first born,
Perpetual maiden, unwed, furnace-dwelling, all-consuming,
Bright-faced goddess of the central hearth within Zeus's hallowed hall.
Ever-burning radiance within the bright home of Apollon,
You who are at the center of every flame, seen and unseen,
To you we start all prayers, you at the beginning of all.

Ares

    Ares is the son of Zeus and Hera. He is a passionate and often volatile god of battles and war. Likewise he is virile, aggressive, and largely unconquerable. Even in love, to which he submits, he is not owned, but rather soothed and calmed by his lover Aphrodite. Ares is the protector of the homeland and the mighty warrior with unquenchable thirst. He is a fierce aid in the battles in which we engage, and a great ally at our side through hardships that we may face.

To Ares
Proud Ares lays at rest, in Aphrodite's golden bower,
Ravaging powerful male, sweetened, can be calmed by tender love.
The Muses sing and cajole to provoke a mighty dance,
The clang of spear and shield rise above to celebrate.
That he join the shout of the company of happy men,
Depart, depart gentle girl, sweet wife and mother women.

Hail Ares ever-vigilant, scanning the dusty perimeter,
Hail giant among gods, the strength of arm protecting.
Let not the wolves at the gates tear away at our race,
To not drench the fields in our innocent children's blood.

The guard at the gate wears proudly his towering helm,
Standing at the gates of our homes, of city, you are guarding.

And when the dogs of war do race, like plagues across the land,
Sound the troops, rouse their warrior spirits with loud cry,
That they go to off to fight, that they go whether to live or die.
May those that would cause us harm tremble before your wrath,
Blood-lusting god, your thirsty sword will drink the blood of men,
To protect the wealth, in family and gem, of our noble land.

Mighty Ares

Bronze-armed Ares, red-cloaked: fire, life and blood,
How heavy your step and the clang of armaments,
An ancient song and dance to raise the heart in men
Like the heartbeat within the earth, pulsing flame
Beating upon the ground and shield, o lusty song.

Unbending, undiverting, level is your gaze on land,
Steel-eyed tempest god, the evil flee before you:
They quake in terror and hide their eyes from your sight,
Fearing the rising wind, the inferno spinning
Those flaming teeth waiting to bite and consume.

Away the evil from the door, Ares stands guard!

Ares II

O Ares, crimson-ribboned, lion-roaring, proud vanquisher,
Fierce god, of splendid and terrifying countenance,
Equally you measure out your force among the race of men,
Every ground and foundation stone carrying your imprinted stance.
In shadowy places fighting relentlessly upon glorious battle grounds,
There you rule, a warrior, a towering guardian, and unconquerable wall,
Shattering the ravenous chains of conflict from an ageless breast,
The enemies, destructive armies, felled and dark banners fall.
Beneath the rains a sigh, terror and pain are washed away
And the land, she smiles as she receives sunlight upon her face,
Revealing the hidden bower where golden Aphrodite waits
Upon a blossom bed where Harmony is born within your embrace.

Artemis

 Artemis is the twin sister of Apollon and daughter of Zeus and Leto, though in Eleusis she was the daughter of Demeter and Poseidon where her temple sits just before the temple of Demeter. She is the free-loving huntress who roams the mountains and forests, nurturer of the young and protector of children and women. As such, girls entering into marriage leave before her their childhood toys and girdles. Like Hestia and Athena, Artemis is a virgin goddess with mythic ties to the Amazons. She embodies all that is wild and independent, and above all she is a huntress pursuing her prey. She is a torch-wielding goddess and ruler of the light of the moon even as she is savior of the people.

Artemis

Artemis, lion-shooter, deer-slayer,
High-crowned goddess, wide-armed mother,
Virgin mother – mother to none and mother to all,
Uplift us, upraise us in your fierce embrace.
A myriad of infants held at your breast
And the sweetened bees are singing at the comb
Nurturing the young with honey upon their lips,
Here are the nymphs at Dionysos' cradle
And the golden elixir nourishes his tongue.
There where the milky ox plowed the earth

With the point of his great horns
Up sprang the leopard in painted guise,
Sustained and flourishing upon the hunt
Where the bronze deer flee before him,
And the lion roars his triumph
Before he gains wings to the skies
To reach the temple of fire and gold.
How the white doe yearns to be of the golden herd
So she runs to be free;
And how the lion dreams of broad eagle's wings
To chase the twin lights of the sun.
High is the arc of your arrow raised
To shoot us like a star flying through the sky;
And the hunting horn, like a spark in the night,
Is lightning in the blood and makes us fly
With dog and bow as our companion and guide.

To Agrotera

Muses grant me voice to sing, nymphs taking up the dance,
Dancing among their midst is slim-ankled Artemis.
The lyre thrums the melody from Apollon's golden hand,
Exotic, wild, is her dance, with her fair-limbed nymphic band.
Dancing through the flowered meadows scented sweet,
Dancing along the rushing deep-voiced river and melodic spring.

Hail to you fair-formed Artemis of the shafts and the bow,
Strong-armed daughter of kindly Leto, beloved child of father Zeus.
The far-ranging mountain boasts to be your happy hollow,
The waterways delight to bathe your hunt-heated flesh,
The many-voiced forest whispers of your pursuit and hunt.
Far-racing goddess, let loose your shining arrows!

Your horn blasts akin to the raging of the long-horned bull,
Hear the hounds raise their voices to its low voiced song.

They strike upon the wind, fleeting shadows in the wood,
And there upon the wooded paths the nymphs race to the hunt.
Flowing tresses ripple, the shout of laughing voices,
But none fairer than thee, Artemis of the shining brow.

Neither night nor day can still your far-treading restless hunt,
Prey falls before you under sun, and the burning torch.
Before your golden bow all beasts flee and quake,
And tender women on childbed call out silent by your dart.
Subdued is the tawny lion, predator turned prey!
Struck down is the stag, so too the doe within the forest glade.

Bloody, slaying goddess, merciful are your sunlit arms
As beasts of wild fall beneath your quick slaughter-hand,
With gentle ministration, you guard and preserve the soft-eyed young.
Though the mother doe falls before you,
Let not our beloved breast be pierced,
But yet take us with your swift-flying arrow when our end is at hand.
Hail to you deadly, merciful Agrotera of the bow and unerring dart.

Artemis at Eleusis

There is a light upon the road
Where the twin torches raised
Lead in a cyclic dance of life
Nodding from their two seats
The double arcs of pointed light.
The radiance of moon and sun
Dancing with their governance
Mark out the timely span
Bound beneath nature's law
Upon the cultivated land.
Souls upon Demeter's road
Where she waits, poppy-crowned
In one hand the flow of seed
In the other the grain of gold
A journey the white dogs keep
Loving guardians of loyalty
Advancing to the huntress' lead,
And bright-sounding Hekate Skilakitis,
To the favored hunt of Artemis.

There the leader of the hounds
Child of solid earth and moving sea
Whom the nymphs of two planes
Keep in swift-footed company
She dances before them all
Across the shadow bridge
Where seven pillars stand
Of frightful gaze that does not deter
The coiled path of the running dogs.
On the road traveling between
The sweet water and the sea
Along the sacred road
The tempered souls travel

As each year marks its round
Their curving road circling around
Like a labyrinth's hidden path
To the altar before the steps
Of the greater gate that awaits
To welcome you initiates.

She stands before the blossom
The flower opened to bloom
With perfect numbered petals firm
And two torches mark the presence
Of where the bright twins reside,
Between their flames the sacrifice
Purified by the grasp of the sea
A mother sacrificed for her progeny
A death to be reborn
The seed that drops
The egg born to new beginning
Before the great gates of Eleusis.
And as a girl, like a bride,
Gives her childhood final respect
To lay her girdle at the altar
Of loud-laughing Artemis,
Here the old misty gowns are laid
Tattered and shorn from their travail
Before the great gates of Eleusis.

Artemis the Purifier

Three ways she glances at the center of purification,
For season of decay has fallen, awaiting her hand,
Before the rest, before new can come, to all things bow.
She shall strike the blow, she shall consume the old,
And the great stag shall be shorn, his blood a river red.

Artemis I submit before you, Artemis I await the strike,
I am at a doorway, I am at the gates of death for this life,
And so I surrender the flesh to you so that I may continue.
There are no tears, the old is like a ghost of what was,
The old is a shadow with pale eyes like a rag on the wind.

And when girlhood has gone away, I lay the toys before you,
At your altar I lay the maiden things and unfasten the maiden's belt,
For I grow to womanhood and prepare for the marriage bed.
I shall be then flushed with light, you happily see me depart,
For you are the transitions of little girls
That they may don the bridal veils.

I have danced for you, and in that dance I have shown my strength,
In that dance I celebrated innocent joys, and prepared
To release the maidenhead,
So at your altar I shall dance once more as a girl
On the brink of womanhood.
I shall be bathed and cleaned in the sacred running pool,
Before I step up to the great stones of your sheltered altar,
And so I shall be flushed with a light that will glow from within,
As I come before your holy high-dancing, far-leaping, fire.

Before you at your altar stone I shall lay a golden lock from my head,
And there the delicate threads, unbound, will be carried on the wind,
Three unraveled sparkling color so faint, bound for places unknown.
A memento this I leave behind, as I leave behind the child's days.

Hail to your bright Artemis,
Purifier by the shining lake and rushing stream,
By the burning flame of your bright shining torch!

Soteira

Lady, Savior, we cry out to you,
The voices of men and women cry out to you,
And the little soft words of children too.
The heavens quiver beneath your silvery steps,
The seas rush forward and back at your caress,
And there the earth reveals to you at your request.

The sea's crashing waves shall not overturn the ship,
In both hands you grasp the bow in your strong grip.
Steady the stern, guide the passage safe within your net,
Lead into welcoming harbor where by Aktaios we shall be met.
Over lands and seas you cross, Soteira you preserve!

That you once swept a girl away, replacing her with roe,
Exchanging for her sad lot; for a girl a tawny doe!
Sad daughters of fortune's fate, blown upon the wind,
You pluck them from the tides of breeze to a sheltered shore.
Soteira guard well the fragile lives of innocent children!

And when the mother strains, under labor of great duress,
The father raises hands and prays for birth's merciful success,
Let not the dart be stained with the mother's life,
Bring forth the torch to flare and be the tender birthing light.
Soothe the wracking pains that tear from within,
Like the cold-water spring wash over her in healing caress.

Soteira, lady, savior, may hunger never strike the people down,
That you guide the well-aimed missile and bless the furrowed ground.
The cattle bleeds their life, so that we may feast, upon the fertile land,
Rain fall down, nurturing rivers flow, to nurse the tender crops.
The river does not dry in its shifting bed, for by Soteira it is led!

Birth of Artemis

O endless night, without the moon or rising sun to shine,
Outside of all time tracked by their measured orbs,
And the ready new life prepared to depart the mother's womb.
Upon the island birthing bed under the palm's shading limb,
Raise the cry of the mother like a primal triumphant song,
Welcome and greet the fruit of the body.

Fragrant cypress, tree maiden, bows her green-tressed head,
To behold the maiden born under the dark starry heaven.
Beasts of forests rise cry in welcome to their mistress,
And the woodland girls, little nymphs, halt their play to listen.
Rushing lullaby of the ocean welcome the babe at your shore,
Dewy drops of flying mist rise forth to greet and caress the newly born.

A light breaks the darkness, soft unflickering light unfailing,
A golden glow arises, like the moon, over the horizon, sweetly sailing,

A crescendo light as she departs with grace from her mother's house.
Bright shining daughter, golden-browed,
Greets her mother with a lusty howl,
A wild clamorous sound against the island's rocks and winds,
And all hunted beasts they shudder at the huntress's dawn risen.

She leapt instantly up, like a velvet-limbed spotted fawn,
A child's bright eagerness lit up her eyes like the summer day sky,
To behold the world around, a wild refuge to which she was birthed.
Greeting the far-spanning heavens and the solid nurturing earth,
All life and breezes tease her youthful senses for adventure that awaits.
So eager to set off, to see what distance hides, but her mother cries.

Most gentle daughter, tender to her mother in the womb and in birth,
Tended to her laboring body to deliver her brother to the earth.
Sweet child, perfumed by nature's design, dripping honey of the spring,
Eases her mother so carefully with the humming song of darting bees.
Daughter of Zeus, cleansed and purified by the ocean's rushing sprays
Is ready to receive and welcome her brother's golden rays.

Artemis of the North

Winter's long season, drifting snow upon the ground,
Cold still air holds the world, and a cry breaks in sound.
Frigid winter air, icy shafts within the lungs,
And a brief sparkle of light upon the snow from a winter sun.
Brightest light, blinding light upon that liquid glass,
And the falling snow swiftly hides the winding path.

Artemis in a winter sleigh, the deer in winter coats,
Flying across the land of ice, gowned in snow.
Hooded in softest white fur, hidden well from sight,
Her arrow is ready for the notch, ready to take flight.
A whisper of sound echoes far, a breathe is loud to the ear,
Time marks well it passing course in the long winter of the year.

The silence of winter is a song of death and its twin, mild sleep,
And the eager predator tracks more desperately the leaping stag.

The smell of winter is clean on the air, purity in its breath,
To greet her is the drowsy pine's scent of winter's green,
A sudden burst of tree-born song, the winter bird rises to sing.
She is balanced on the edge, a living shadow on the snow,
And the aged bull stiffens as if foreseeing death from the holy arrow.
Winter is harsh for the living, old and weak are seized by its touch,
And the divine huntress leaps in chase in her ageless hunt.

The old one sinks deep into the snow, staining the purity of white,
Captured by the goddess, feast of meat from the sacred site.
Merciful huntress, friend of men – by your arrow we rise and live
To clothe us in the furs to protect us from the harsh winter wind,
To feed our families from the flesh that your blessings send!

Hephaistos

According to some sources Hephaistos is a son begotten solely by Hera, and according to others he is the son of Hera and Zeus. He is the lame god with his twisted foot mythically attributed to Zeus who threw him off Olympos. He is the god of blacksmiths, a forger who creates with his own hands forms including the armor and weaponry of the gods. Perhaps because of his deformity, he is far from a solemn god; instead he is, on his mule, the first among the procession of Dionysos welcoming the presence of the god. He is a god who brings good humor with him.

Hymn to Hephaistos

Cone-crowned Hephaistos, igneous god, wondrous architect—
You own the four corners of the column that naught may fall,
Yours are the four columns of the world to support us all
And you bring all things to their beauty when their time has come.
From the caterpillar's dormant bed, the butterfly flies in its stead
And by the mix of love, a bright-girdled child is formed and bred
As such as when from the high crown of father Zeus's head,
That he beseeched to you by your skill bring end or mend
That terrible agony—that piercing, burning misery,
You brought the bright-armored maiden by your wedge
And out she sprung in her raiment gold, armor-clad,
From where you took hold and made the singular mold
Of her vestments in fine detail and splendor your craft did lend
That Athena ever did trust to tend, Klytotekhnes of glorious hand.

Guardian of the forge, you who capture the fire within
Master of forms, the holy substance in your hands bends
That mercurial shape forged in the hot furnace heart
Hephaistos, harnesser of horses, god of industrious hands
Raise the hammer and grasp the tong, Polyphron!
Shape the thing of its ore, the delicate glass from its sands.

Mask-carver, uproarious, reveling, gentle-handed god
You sculpt the egg from sweet water and fertile land
And each infant face so perfectly made by your design
We greet you, nature's foremost and prized artisan
Khaire Polytechnes of hue and line, builder from the pine,
Your hand touches all in our diversity: of plant, of beast and man.
Loud-laughing god encircled by flame and soot
Let your furnace continually billow bright and hot!

Hephaistos II

Bringer of beauty, capturer of beauty
Drawn upon your potter's wheel,
Beauty fired in the breath of your kiln
For all molded by your hands is beauty still.
All captured in your embrace is beauty,
The fairest face is creation of your design
As Pygmalion molded beneath his hands the stone
To sculpt the panes; loveliness for which you pine.
You draw out your heart with all you create,
A fair lover born within the heat of your flame
So each creation bears your kiss, all one and same.

With fair eye you took to your wife Aphrodite,
She who fashions the sweet-face girl into the bride,
The starry-eyed goddess of a thousand forms,
That goddess born on the changeable tide,
Morpho of the golden orb—of the ornate gown,
But you cannot grasp her between your hands
Though you may drape her with golden braids
As she flows, like wind across the sands
Like the sweet river, ever toward her love
And your woven net but holds her light imprint
Of that fairest form you have not wrought
But your match in beauty of unparallel art;

We take your hands as we draw our breath
And let us to her loving embrace we ascend
Between you, you hold that golden thread.

Hephaistos III

How joyously you labor beneath your leather smock
And effortlessly your sparking hammer falls;
Too, the molten metals mold evenly between your hands
You who delight in every shape of life, significant and small
And within the shell you have wrought, you place the iron clock
To time life, as the babe on four shaky legs happily crawls
To become a youth uplifted and spry on the steady pair
And the gnarled limbs that necessitates a third when old age calls
As the sphinx once sang to Oedipus, your great blue print of man
This is all as you have designed, and with humor planned
That form is always changing: bud, bloom and seed in your hand
A masterpiece designed, as you carve the theatric masks of life
Each expression imprinted in supple material, between joy and strife
And how uproariously you laugh as fluid Dionysos exchanges
    one
        after
            one.

Hera

Wife of Zeus and daughter of Rhea and Kronos, Hera is the heavenly queen. First among the gods to marry, she is the goddess who presides over marriage and mother of all. She is a goddess who is everywhere in the air and associated with the rains, as is symbolized by the cuckoo bird that is sacred to her, a form taken by Zeus to lure his bride. The peacock, another bird sacred to her, has the hundred eyes that are mythically said to have guarded Io in the form of a cow. Mythically portrayed as a jealous wife, Hera sets the stage of Heroism, such as with the labors of Herakles.

Hymn to Hera

O queenly Hera, crowned with five-point flowers, Antheia,
Starry goddess, great of power, born of proud ancestry,
Fair bearer of the blooming branch, the apples of Esperides,
Delightful tender of the garden, you royal honeybee,
The pure pearls of honey drip from your pale fingertips
Mixed with the rains that fall so sweet from heaven to sea,
Nursemaid and High Mother of the world and all!

Airy goddess of perfumed arms, the breath and wind your charms
Wreathed in sacrificial smoke in which you delight.
Hyperkheiria, your magnificent hand stretches over the sky
Protect us from harm; curb the ravages of ceaseless plight
As the oak with mighty arms holds the ravenous wind at bay
And though the course may darken all the day to night
Deliver us, stately Queen of the ever-living hall!

Hymn to Hera Aigophagos

Aigophagos, statuesque goddess of the stripped goatskin hide,
Cleansing goddess, purifier, you hold the straps in your grip
And the twisted horns we adorn on your lofty altar, raised to the sky
To you who have set the trials that must be passed to advance
The girl to be the bride, and the boy to be the honorable man
That we may drop the girdles and locks of our youth,
And be adorned anew.

As Herakles followed the road that you led, never far from your side
The glorious son fought and won, on the road set by your fingertip,
Came to rest in the heart of the Lakedaimia to be cleansed and purify
The guilt of guest-blood from his hands, he who bore his consequence.
But Oionos closed his youthful eyes by the sons of Hippokoon
And when Herakles delivered his wrath, there you were in kindly hue

That aided and unfettered he slew, and offered humble gifts to you
And so we also do, whether we be many, or we be few.

We honor you, righteous goddess, that in absolute fairness you stand;
Trial-leader to you we submit, submit to your firm hand,
You who receive the shorn goat's horns at the trial's end

Hera

Between the light and misty remains
Of crystalline drops of heavenly rains,
The form of which to your messenger imbues
Gentle and swift, fair Iris of myriad hues,
A bright arch, your bridge across the sky
For your gentle rain, as if the heaven in joy did cry,
Brings your beauteous gifts upon the earth
The blushing flowers reaching up from the stony girth.
For never more do the larks so sweetly sing
Than after the silvery cuckoo shakes his wings,
And the raindrops falling from his feather-tips
To land upon your children's parted lips.
In these fashions you send us your motherly love
Delivered in plenty from the bright sky above.

To Hera

Muses join me upon the hill, and lift your harmonious voices high
As we sing to the goddess, golden-browed, Hera, heavenly queen.
She who sits high-throned in the company of the radiant gods,
And is adored by the great-plumed, bright-crested birds at her hand.
Hail to the heavenly queen who blesses the marriage-bed,
And there the morning-dewed bride receives the nuptial kiss.

Revered goddess, hear the songs and prayers of women who entreat,
Accept the welcomed place of honor at our home and hearth.
Your own house receives you, and will tremble before your might,

And too you ease the head of your spouse against your pillowed breast.
Most honorable Hera you are strong-armed among gods and men,
Your will rises like a lioness from the earth's plumage draping the land.

As terrible as your might, you coax with your honeyed tongue,
The wearied husband to your fragrant arms upon the mountain peak.
And there with Aphrodite's grace, do your extend your loving embrace,
Amends are made and cordiality restored between husband and wife.
Good counselor of the king among gods and men, veiled goddess,
Your utterance commands the attention of all in great assembly.

Hyperkheiria, your hand extends throughout the heavens arch,
The stars and moon in orbit shine upon your heavenly form.
The hours, days and passing seasons bring forth your holy cup,
As you swallow the great libations that pass through your pearly lips.

To Hera II

Khaire Hera, robed in azure, gowned in the summer sky
And the diamonds hang at your nimble fingertips
Embroidered with silver at the hem, like refreshing rain
Winking rainbows merrily to the white face of the sun
As you are touched tenderly at the hand by shining Apollon;
Hail to you mountainous queen, far-flying, broad-winged
Goddess of dewy succor, unshakable mother of all,
At our altars you mix with the rising smoke of the incense
As your kindly breath stirs the trembling offerings of the holy trees,
Wafting the primal element to mix with the burning laurel leaves;
Mother of Olympia, you extend your arms in fair embrace
 From your high seat, you who govern the children of the race,
You who greet the daphne-crowned winner of the holy game,
You greet your wearied children from their trials, one and same;
Hail to you royal queen, lapis-crowned wife of Zeus!

Poseidon

Poetically called one of the three Zeuses (Zeus, Hades and Poseidon), Poseidon rules the in-between world of the seas. His temples on the coast overlooked harbors of naval fleets and those of fishermen. Like Zeus and his son Apollon, Poseidon has oracular associations and according to some myths once presided over Delphi, before Delphi became the oracle of Apollon. The horse, an important vehicle, belongs to Poseidon. In one version of the myth, horses were created as a gift to Demeter, in another the horse was created in contest with Athena. In addition to being the god of the sea, he is also the earth-shaker.

To Poseidon

As a dark-flecked stallion follows the mare at the edge of the sea,
So do the winding songs of the Muses follow short behind,
To sing of dark-maned Poseidon of the turbulent crashing wave.
The craggy sea-edge is a quiet noisy place, suspense hangs in air,
Hear now wanderers along its banks the deep voice of pounding reef.
The scaling rocks give way to a soft welcome sandy shore,
Where goddesses in splendor under sunlight play and gently sleep.
The tide has fingers that draw against the earth, push and caress,
In that meeting place raging sea kisses coaxingly the parting land.
Coral-crowned Gaieokhos there did spy Demeter of the golden rows,
Such was his eager love that he fashioned for her with great care,
A splendid guise swift of foot and neck proud arched for her to ride.
Eager to woo her, eager to claim, but all for not, a purpose lost in vain.
The wide-armed earth does not submit to oceanic demand.
To Olympos he arises, but to a watery domain he rules and sets to rest,
Amid the currents of the belt of Okeanos spanning from east to west.
A watery home in the bosom of the ocean tides, in monstrous company,
A coral castle shining bright, and there nereids play, at the heart of sea.
Hail to you mighty Pelagaios, ruling the far-reaching currents and tides,
To you who raise the violent crashing waves to devour the coastal lands.

Under the deceptive calm of fair waves, your trident strikes the earth,
Trembling all in your embrace, great shocks leap and wrack the land.

But temper soothed how calm you become and kindness you extend,
Prayers rise up from the traveler's mouth, Hail to you Asphalios!
A prayer for far-traveling kindly winds, O securer of the voyages safe.
You rock the boat with gentle lull, waves do not violently toss it about,
And the flowing sea rises in the night like a sweet-singing melody.
How men have yearned and loved the foamy-tressed melodic daughters,
And hid their faces in respect to your tempest-raising crowned sons.
But fear and awe shakes them for sharp-jawed monsters of the deep,
That your power shall shackle and lead,
Astride your magnificent ocean-born stallion steed.

Prayer to Poseidon

(Boat Upon the Sea)

Poseidon, king of the middle space, of the rolling sea
Where the waves carry the voyagers to our destiny;
There on Poseidon's sea the painted boat is sailing,
Eyes fixed to the horizon where ocean meets heaven
And a guiding map for the aware mind rises high
We are moved upon the sea by the breath of the sky.
A fair wind may carry us upon calm sea in tranquility,
There where stillness may forge weary chains of captivity
Or the violent breeze draws us upon the battling sea
And upon thunderous crests the foamy mares pull this chariot
Whether to meet wreckage and ruin in the sea's embrace
Or find triumph by our hearts and immortal grace.
O Poseidon, to you we pray to not be conquered by the wave
That the perils that rest between the pull of earth and heaven
Not become so great as to drag us down to our destruction
So we may arrive past the storm, to the shores of destiny.

Poseidon in Winter

Expanse of ocean, breadth of sea
Rolling, rising within wintry beds
There the ice-licked waves crest
The salt breath upon a deserted beach.
There Poseidon rides the turning slope
Drawing the crashing waves to and fro
Echoing against the emptiness
With frigid kisses upon the shores.
Frosted brine and powdered snow
Like a lover in the dark, returning again
To draw the embrace of the Earth
And plant the moist seed within.
Poseidon embraces Demeter in wide arms
By the shore and expanse of land
Midnight passions of the sea
To draw from the earth a new beginning
To stir the sleeping maiden, beloved of three.

Father Sea

Father Sea I hear you calling,
The rushing waves sing against the rock.
The echo of water crashing to stone,
And there I hear my sisters in the hollowed wind.
A risen song echoing against the rocky slope,
Welcoming, welcoming the sister to the fold.
Join in dance beloved sisters among the waves,
Dance for Father Sea who yields plenty to all.
Father Sea who shakes the rounded earth,
Shakes from it firm wide-spanning grasp,
Violent waves ebb away the fragile sloping shore.
The sea draws away in foamy arms stone from stone,
And casts earth's richness to the life of the seas.
Regeneration – all things spring from old anew!
Father Sea I hear your loving words,
A haunting melody of a midnight calm,
Across a moving glass, reflecting heavenly glow.
Father, Father I hear you call out to me,
My heart sings a melody of the dancing sea.
And if I listen in silence that best receives,
I can hear your song in the dolphin's company.
Concealing seas, hidden away and hidden deep,
A bright flame burns within the heart of the sea.
Restless flames that stirs the ocean beds,
Heat rises, life rises and a birth is formed.
Little island set adrift among the rocking waves,
A soothing cradle for your head – and father loving.
Sea winds bring sustenance to sow within so deep,
Into the furrows of richest, dark, welcoming soil,
No barren rock thrust from his loving heart,
But a paradise to mature and to fruition grow!
Father Sea I come to you upon my little boat,
The waves part welcoming before my path,

Traveling, boat unturned by threat of rolling storm,
Through you I am balanced upon turbulent rise,
Rise and rest among the foamy mare's backs,
But never to fall, to sink within the briny seas.
Death does not happily seek me from my father's throne,
He does not eagerly seek death in the house,
Drag into death into the dark waters deep.
Father Sea I embrace you – touch your rising arms,
Again and again I return to a father's embrace,
Rejuvenate the spirit, happy as the gull's merry clatter,
Who drifts upon the sea-churned winds, lofty waves.
No hunger shall I ever yearn, for plenty is what you provide,
The fruits of the seas shall ever in my heart sustain me,
My brothers and sisters nurture me on these simple feasts.
A simple feast, not to be under-valued, its richness is within.
Father Sea I come to you, you carry freedom so sweet,
Far away to distant lands, no boundaries for your might,
Yet however far I travel upon your wide-trekking mounts,
However the distances may bring to me rise and rest again,
Carry me always again, to bring me welcoming home,
To the home that forever lights that fiery lamp,
That dwells within the ocean of my wandering heart!

Athena

Athena is the daughter of Zeus, born without mother from the head of her father. She is the embodiment of wisdom, knowledge and strategy. She is unwaveringly loyal to her father and often carries out the will of Zeus. She is a goddess who patronizes teachers, and a goddess who is often at the aid of heroes on their journeys. The olive, a plant that gives precious oil as a trade commodity as well as its fruits, was given to mankind by Athena in her contest with Poseidon. She is the honorable warrior and knight. Athena is also the goddess of the fiber arts, particularly weaving. She binds to create something new and durable. She is honored alongside both Hephaistos and Apollon.

Hymn to Athena
Upon your loom you weave the cloth's immortal design
Drawn of myriad hues and colors unknown to mortal eyes.
Everlasting weaver, goddess who holds the needle,
Patient gatherer of the hundred thousand threads
Concealed beneath your veil, impenetrable one,
Bird singer, Aegean-eyed goddess, your father's delight,
Straight oak standing with strength and solidity,
Pull the threads to their equal measure
And bind them to the unconquerable shaft,
As Dionysos was bound once to his father's thigh.

There the pole has gathered to point the way
And you lift your triumphant spear to greet the sky.
Horse driver, measured speaker, honorable warrior,
Bright-armored Athena, indestructible unwavering maid,
Let the golden shine of your armor and helm be our aid
You, adorned and born in the glory of your immortality.

To Athena

Guardian of the gates of the foundation, of greatest learning,
You proudly stand before entrance, at the arc of the door.
Unconquerable Athena, guard well the mind's great sanctuary
That each student passes safe beneath your steady gaze,
And every teacher reminded of their great responsibility
As all come beneath the shadow of your shield and spear upraised.
You are present within every hall, between every wall,
The learned and the seeking all receiving your divine blessing,
For they nurture and hone that great treasure within,
And fill the mind with cleverness, logic and skills of reasoning,
To think deftly and plan, to lead and not be led,
To weave the facts into a great masterpiece.
And there the relationships from beginnings we see,
All things are connected—an impact like a ripple on the sea.
Bestow your blessings upon those who teach and those who learn,
And that the gates of knowledge stand well-armed,
To push back those that would seek to tear down the wall,
Driving men toward ignorance of the darkest days.
Beneath your hand the hallowed towers stand tall,
And a million voices speak out from the ages past and old,
Passing forward the wisdom of ancestors from one age to new.

To Athena II

Calm-eyed Athena, even-voiced, just goddess,
Kind goddess, gentle wind of aid to the hero's quest,
Chalinitis, harnesser of horses, you who tamed Pegasus
That strong-willed Bellerophon may find swift wings to fly
Who found his trial by Chimera's fire and the Solymoi tribe.
By your fingertip you uplift the greater portion
Of the crushing weight: our trial, our happy burden,
Ever as you stand beside us, both the gentle and the bold
That we are given the exact measure of what we can hold,
As once by your fingernail you uplifted heaven's dome
For mighty Herakles as Atlas between sky and stone.
You are the kind friend walking across the land
Unwearyingly, wise daughter of Zeus, councilor of man
You are with us with victory perched upon your hand.

To Athena III

Bright goddess, friend of Necessity, mother of invention,
Far-seeing Ergane, deliverer of your finest arts,
Once you drew the air across the reed to create
The shepherd's modest pipes, in which Pan takes delight,
Crying the haunting song of the immortal soul,
A melody born between the balance of air and land.
And there the olive sprouts between your toes,
Branching up from the foot of your regal seat,
By virtue of which the spark is fed on the oil lent light
And nurturing young and old, generations manifold,
Living beneath the shadow of your administering hand.
May our minds bear the creative light, to renew the self again
To carve new roads, and sing our souls; to feed our minds
That we may not in one place stand, but we ever rise.

Aphrodite

Goddess of love, beauty and peace, Aphrodite was born from the foam when Zeus castrated Kronos and threw his reproductive organs into the sea. She is the lover of Ares to whom she bore many children, and wife of Hephaistos. One famous lover of Aphrodite is Adonis. Her mourning of his death is celebrated annually by her worshippers. She is the goddess of brides, gowning them and crowning them in preparation for their weddings. She is Morpho, the goddess of changing forms as one enters from girl to wife. As goddess of peace and harmony she is the goddess too of doves. As the ruler of love she is both a caring goddess and one who is highly offended by those who reject her area of ruling.

Sonnet for Aphrodite

Starry mother of the mortal Nation,
You tore the seed from the ruby stamen
Yoking conflict of might for creation
In the flower bed bore by gentle women.
Your lover dons his triumphant circlet
And his sword lies lax. Silent in love's arms
He rests his head, subdued by Eros' net
And fiery war surrenders to your charms.
The fire shall bow to justice and to peace,
Where spring's new poppies will be blushing red,
For by your hand all strife will calm and cease,
And all your children raise their hopeful head.
O Aphrodite, mother, where is she?
Where is your golden daughter, Harmony?

To Aphrodite

Muses grant me a fair voice to sing, worthy of perfumed Aphrodite.
Aphrodite dwells within her golden house, crowned and adorned,
Her honeyed fingers stretch forth to sway the lover's embrace,
All honor to her, ruler of the hearts, and to you all men adore.
Hail to you Aphrodite, your tresses bound with the ivory comb.
All Honor to you Aphrodite, upon your head rests the golden crown.

Limpid-eyed Anaduomene, your body is the foam that bore you forth,
The kiss of moisture, as morning dew upon the spanning earth.
Your breath is blossom sweet, as you whisper into our souls,
Rousing the heated flame from the sparked kindling of passion burning.
Gold is the arrow that sparks our hearts, drawing us into sweet embrace,
And lead is the arrow that turns our hearts, away in dread and pain.
By your hands these arrows you craft, and set into the fair-hued quiver,
Send upon the heavens your bright-eyed son, deliver your will to men.

Bless the marriage bed, craft not an arrow to lead loving hearts astray,
And to sweet youth bring the first bloom of romance with gentle hand.
Let your art strike our spirits, Ourania, with heavenly gods-blessed love.
Let the dart rouse our flesh and hearts, Pandemos, and bring us bliss.

Aphrodite

O sweetest elixir of life, clinging to dewy petals
And blooms between the sun and moon
Where the pearls of the sea tumble upon the shores,
So lovingly kissed by pale foam
That moisture of twilight adorns its mistress' brow
With seduction's fragrance certain to allure
A mating musk that entwines, brings together
And joins hearts of mortals and divine.
In her power, Aphrodite cannot be denied,
That sweet romance bent on seducing
Touching upon hearts that she sees, that fertile ground
Eros' dart would shortly seize,
Try to turn away your face and there again she is,
Wafting the perfume, ensnaring the senses
Enchanting your heart with lover's arms,
And the heated lips that draws you to the game,
For Aphrodite is playing with forms, to attract and delight,
To weave love's net born aloft
To captured hearts by her blessed gift,
Her child of union on timeless wings.

Apollon

Apollon is the twin brother of Artemis, and son of Leto and Zeus. He is the oracular god who speaks the will of Zeus, a god of healing, of music and poetry, the leader of the muses, and god of light. His various epithets include Loxias (the god who delivers the right word of Zeus), and Lykeios (of light). Apollon is a god who brings with him logic, reason, freedom and liberty. He is associated with Helios, the sun, and is described as the god with the unshorn locks of gold hair much like the rays of the sun. The laurel is sacred to him and is awarded to winners of competitions.

To Apollon

Muses nine, to divine melody in orbit they dance,
As would the electrons about the nucleus,
The song of order, that turning rhythm,
Deathless song of life, of all the ages.
Seven in number, their voices flying on ribboned wings,
The seven swans they forever sing,

The children of Apollo, bedecked in their father's golden light,
Purity, earth, heaven and sea between day and night.
And too the five member chorus,
Numbered groups of maidens and of boys,
The procession of youth, beautifully,
Singing praises to Apollo, son and king.

Double ram-horned, at the edge of the sea,
Apollo wears the crown of divinity,
From where the horns flame in golden light,
Spiral up the twisting cornus.
O Pan among the meadows, at side of the lusty-voiced herds and flocks,
Where music whistles upon the errant breeze
Through the syrinx's slender reeds.
And here at the coastal sea, where the caverns run deep,
All hail under the auspicious day and night beneath the full moon light
Honored with the poets sweet lyric, with choral song and dance,
Hail to the bright-browed god of the ram's spiraled horn,
Sing to the august Apollo.

Where the land meets the water's crest,
The children of the sea give tribute
And the whistling song of a hundred dolphins rise from the foam,
Dancing like bejeweled sparks of light upon the crystalline wave,
To join the mortal weave upon the festive loom.
Fibers woven in sacred dance, strong brilliant threads
Of love, laughter, voice and song, spun bright threads
Of the light of freedom in the hearts of humanity weaving its tapestry,
A delicate cloth, burning bright,
The golden veil rising to the heavens high.
That gossamer veil of light Apollo receives and dons,
That story of his children's love.

Solar King

The Muses sing in adoration beyond the heavens high
Where the sun, mightily crowned, sits upon his flaming throne,
Bearing his scepter in hand uniting all the worlds
That orbit at his breadth, bathed in his majesty.
The pulse of his song turns the spheres in harmony,
For where the worlds circle round vibrates upon the lyre strings,
To whom Helios yields, Apollo the bright-eyed solar king!

Outside and of all time he is plucking the strings of solar song,
And the stars they are dancing so far beyond to that melody
Each star his own kingdom and brother to another,
In truth all joined in unity.
He is the great king in his own kingdom to where his light extends,
But among the high powers of the galaxy the throne yields to its level
For the deathless ones rise higher above what is beyond.

Here in limitless place the sun is but another son, shining star
Wreathed in the brightest light of gold and red upon his unshorn head,
A prince of fairness and grace, speaking the laws of universal word
Upon the thousands of million thrones bearing his shining torch.
O glorious Apollo dancing in divine radiance across dark space,
You are rejoiced upon the living lips of many, and within our hearts.

Our earthly view we see him day and night, that bright-armed light
The luminous far-reaching beams chase dark-eyed night to her bower
And the nocturnal stars lighting from worlds beyond
Upon their lofty towers.
Beloved son of Zeus, light reborn in every vibrant flush of morn
Maturing in a breath of time, he rises by swift mares into heaven's arch.
East to rise, west to descend, the flaming mares fly
His route heralded by a great symphony painted across the sky.

Phoebus, light upon the earth, you mark our day and hour,

To your song all the seasons and days do merrily dance,
Sister yielding to the rule of another, honored above in the Muses song.
All earthly life bows before you, and nature bends her head to your gift
For when the spring light touches the sleeping soil it raises life
And when rosy-faced winter shakes her heavy white gown
There you are beyond the horizon, at the edges of the world,
Most beloved and regal light all vegetation rises and rests to your crown!

But light expands beyond our world and beyond all the worlds next
Far-reaching god, fire-adorned, you are here and at a distance
Earthly and enthroned so far beyond,
You are the son, the prince and king
That from your throne you receive and pass the mantle of order down,
From universe to galaxy, through the tall towered heavens,
To the place where it is delivered –
Where the light touches the living ground!

To Pythios

Musegetes turn favorable regard upon me as I sing of the gods this day,
For I sing of you great Apollon
Who bears the instruments of purification.
And there beneath your golden foot disease and plague does lay,
There the mighty serpent lies bloodied, dead and slain.
Vanquisher of the foul I sing to you, who drive plague from the door,
A sacrifice that renews, the blood of the dead
Becomes the speaking river.
Hail Apollon, mighty is the sword, the bow and the flying arrow,
And those shafts of light that devoured the torn flesh of Python,
May they consume and bring to waste the ills harbored within men all.

That which you touch you do strip bare before you,
That which you see is completely revealed in your emanation,
Maddened pestilence, bringer of foul offerings, lays exposed.
Your hand does wield the arrow and sword which drives it forth,
And your light penetrates all, to rot the bloated venomous serpent.
And there the voices rise to sing
From the throats of women and men alike
To Pythios, destroyer of the predator pestilence that feasts
The serpent with a thousand mouths that snap upon us.
Rejoice in the death of the plague to men and his beasts,
The devourer has been shorn of his teeth and claws
And lies now as dust beneath you.

To Loxias

A song is woven of instruments' voice, woven tight with chosen words,
And the words may be sung alone, unaccompanied, from a valley or rise,
For their power does weave the threads of hymn
Lifting aloft to the skies.
Muses, great art smiths of the words, lend to my talent your divine aide,
To rightly sing of the God of Word
To whom we all who lift voices owe.

Hail Loxias, you are the Word of your Father
Ushered from untainted lips,
And like the crash of light from his bolt,
You swiftly descend gold-adorned,
A voice spiraling up from the cavern within—
Bring the Word to the race of men.

And through that cavern your waters flow,
Never ceasing from their source,
The speaking river utters the words,
As it turns upon its ceaseless course.
Water rises up, the words rise up within,
And is delivered to the race of men.
Loxias, true-speaking, most honored god
Raised beside the prophetic seat,
The oracles created of your Word
Are a glimmer in the history dusts,
Where once you reigned golden-crowned,
And surveyed your land as hawk in flight,
Seeing in all directions, knowing of all directions
That have been lain to ground.
Woven fate is a giant unfolding tapestry,
Hanging on a great loom,
As neighboring threads do touch
In the directions of their course, so you see,
And so you know, and by the will of Zeus who sees all,
You deliver to our own.
Those oracle seats are empty,
Touched by ancient dust from the kind hands of age,
But still you speak to those who may listen and who may hear!

But O lord Apollon; see the false prophets
Like serpents plentiful on the ground,

In pretense to sit in your most holy seat,
To falsely wear the Pythians' crown.
You see them there draped in their own splendor,
And in silence wait the time,
For the gods do not forget transgressions
That mortal pride does make.
An arrow is notched for each of them,
Who in vanity of their glory give false words,
They bask in the honors risen up to esteem of men,
Unearned and undeserved.
The serpent dart will come to strike down
The far-reaching pride to the dusty ground,
And your children shall rejoice
When you have toppled vanity from the deceitful throne.

Hail Loxias, we listen silently,
For your Words are spun in the world all around,
Yours is the lauded voice
That of which all of nature speaks and owes,
And truth you utter from gentle lips,
Humble and surrendered to your embrace.
I do not believe that the oracles speak no more,
But that the words are in fair grace,
Spoken from those you touch and claim,
And make your mark upon their crown.
Fair lips speak in truth, not be tainted with deceit
And lies to disgrace your gift,
And there the oracle shall speak,
Your Word moving as water through earth,
A course is carved and the chosen submits,
Away from corruption at your hearth.

To Lykeios

In the night is the eerie song
Fracturing the silence into a hundred shards
The night cracks with the streams of faint light
As the green and rosy hues of the borealis
Rival the frosty breath of dawn.
The wolves, my brothers, are singing
They are calling in their sacred choir
As the world is wrapped in shadows
And their eyes are gems of fire
They are beckoning to you in the early hour
In the edge of the winter
O return now the bright dawn,
Death's blood of winter stains the ground
And the world slumbers on,
O return now the bright dawn.
Lykeios, you are the shifting light
First light, wolf light
The blue shine of your eyes
Are as the morning and evening star
Cutting the darkness with your brilliant glare,
And there you are traveling over the snow
So blinding is the white coat you wear
Where each strand refracts
The prism of hues locked within the pallor.

I am there among the wolves
My heart runs their light-footed race
A winged rhythm dancing within my soul
My lungs draw in the sharp air
And my lips loosen the primeval song
From the hidden places in my soul,
Song of beginnings
As I join the eerie choir
In those days before the dawn.

Apollon Hyperborean

Hail to you Apollon, you who have donned
The swan-feather cloak, soft plumes and down
You who are crowned in fine white rays of light
You departed your seat as day yields to night;
And about your wrist you wrapped five times
The ribbon of soft hue, dyed in another clime,
As your left hand grasps tenderly the lyre of gold
You are singing the days like a minstrel of old.
By the familial fireside your radiant light throws
The dancing figures born of the shadows
And by a whisper you create a world by song
You storyteller, sharing your boundless love
At your winter seat, you king of the Hyperborean.

Apollon of the North

Upon the ice we dance among the gods,
All honor beating of eternity upon primal drum,
In the land of the darkest winter night
And eternal summer light we sing to Apollon
Where the days do not measure
And an echoing stillness stretches on.
Here the ocean finds its port,
A jagged harbor rising proud from the rocky ground,
Where the ancients sing a hollow groan,
A timeless song, as the ice falls into the sea,
A land where the great whales sing,
A rumble of thunder through the water,
Here they gather to greet the golden Lord
Who sets his foot upon the risen shore.
From a land where the glacier walks
With his furrowing steps from time's beginning,
Singing his slow-moaning rasp of deep tone,
The songs of his labor's tread.
All is music in this furthest north,
The chimes of the wind against the horns of ice,
And some silence of purity is a strangest melody;
A movement of light, creating song,
That here the aurora dances amid the heavens
In array of light for a symphony;
Each finger of color is a note of sound
Within the heart calling to ancestors of old.
Upon that night rainbow he draws it up to a cloak
And dances upon its fluid road,
See there in the heavens where he rides
That rolling tide of color across the sky.
In this land on the edge of time
Apollo wears his icy crown where shining prisms reside,
Radiating all the colors of dancing light

Rising to heaven from the earth,
Here he wears all the light, crowned of heaven
And draped in silvery shining velvet.
Lo he wreathes his brow with a hundred stars
Shining as the white-fire of the forge,
And the earthly stars, crystalline sculpted ice
Within the blanket of heavenly snow,
Lying across the broad-breasted land
Is an ethereal glow where his footsteps touch.
Where day arises as an arch
Over the crest of land to quickly descend,
Here the bright purity of life colors the sky
The crispest blue to fall into vivid gold.
Night reclaims for her own the winter-land,
Nurturing within her timeless arms,
And upon her wintry-pure breast Apollo rests his head,
Brightest light of the night,
His voice threaded into the endless music
Woven within that stillness of time and space,
Enthroned upon the endless heavens and the chiseled earth-
Land of water, stone and ice!

Apollon at Mycenae

There is Apollon like the lion
With his crowning mane
Like a flame of many rays
Set upon his regal brow
And fresh bloom of flowers
Are woven upon his flowing locks.
The land where he steps
Expands like mellowed gold
Against the mountain peaks
Like gentled dragons sleeping
Beneath the stride of his foot,

Guardians of ancient stone,
Harboring between the stretches
Of their tails
The hidden roads of time past
Upon those which Apollon waits.
He stands at the great gate
Where the dancing pride
Of his regal lionesses await.

For The Noumenia

Noumenios rises with the newborn month,
Tracking the passage of time,
Bearing in hand his silver bow, like the crescent in the sky pale lit.
Selene rises from the waves, water trailing from her silver locks,
See how her silver crescent rises,
The winged drawn cart into the heavenly arch.
Hail Noumenios above, your light turns the succession of days,
And before you the moon withers and fills,
Marked upon Selene's pearly breast.

Apollon of the unshorn locks,
You rise anew and kindle your flame in your golden house,
Rise into the heavens dripping dew,
Newly born rising into the flush of man.

Hail bright crowned Selene, rekindling your own flame,
Shining with borrowed light,
High we see the bull's horns that curve
Upon your fair-tressed head so bright.
White-armed goddess, we greet your pale form in splendor,
Lifting into heavens high,
Mother of time's passage, the dancing daughters,
Months, and fair-faced seasons.

Hail to you mother and father of the shining month,
On this night newly begotten,
May she greet us who sing praises,
In fair form and deliver forth a token blessing.
We greet and celebrate the new month,
Selene's laughing-eyed daughter,
Hail to you who brings time passage churning,
And light the heavens renewing.

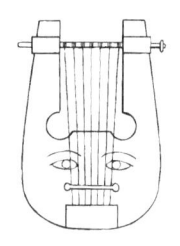

Song of Pyanepsia

The chorus of the snowy mute swans lifts sweetly in song,
As they gather on wing to depart for other lands,
And there the song-birds from the trees sing farewell, farewell to thee.
The trees are stretching up their boughs, fire and light crowned,
Most highly among them beloved Daphne and Athena's olive,
Their leaves shake in a melody to sing to the departing song,
That by their grace at our homes, they will retain his blessings here,
Crowned most beautifully in the fire, and white heavenly light.

O faded light, you see below the children, who lift their arms,
You hear their songs rising up like the small winged birds,
So sweet is the child's little voice, the clear ring of innocence.
They raise up in their hands to you the little crowned bough,
The little child parades it around, to the house where it shall rest,
Where it shall be set with honor by those little hands.

To the feast is carried the eresione, an honored guest for Apollon,
For that branch that bears his light comes all adorned to the table side,
Where the simple feast is set, a feast of warmth in winter's pre-dawn,
There where the night is dark of light, wisdom shall not be forgotten.
The heavy-laden vine has been shorn, and everywhere the bean adorns,
The little bounty that in longevity lasts
Throughout the months of winter cold,
To feed the people where the waning sun
Does not rest and nothing grows.
And so for the feast the beans are gathered for the coming night,
At our hearths that we may retain the light,
Offering up the meal of beans.
To share what we have with you, in that warmth of the boiled brew,
As men have done from some time so long ago, to thank your grace,
First offerings of the fruits your light nourished well,
A hundred thanks to him.

We sing to you, as the light departs, as the sun sinks earlier in the day,
All of the trees and all the mountains have turned to gold,
And the leaves of flaming color loosen their hold
On the slumberous branches.
The winds draw the little tree flames behind you in a train,
Riding the currents of the northern winds that blow winter's dance.
How splendid and beautiful your departing light,
As away the griffin flies,
There the sparks of fire from the chariot wheels
Catches the clouds to such color,
That the heavens are dyed the beauty of all the heavens
In purple, red, and gold.
Those clouds they fan from the wing-beats of the hound of Zeus,
The griffin arises to crest the mountain side,
Hear the autumn thunder roll,
It echoes our melody as we all sing our prayers to you,
Whom all humanity loves,
To await your return from lands of Hyperborean
And bring the dawn again.
All below you call out; Hail to you adorned
In highest pure light, lord Apollon!

Dance of Flowers

Women dancing to your lyre, like butterflies to the fire
We dance for you, O Apollon.
Lifting our baskets up high, raising flowers to the sky
We dance for you, O Apollon.

In our fair hands we will lift, bearing to you a loving gift
We bring a gift to you, O Apollon.
Bringing forth the fairest veil, dyed as morning's sail
We bring a gift to you, O Apollon.

Women dancing to your lyre, like butterflies to the fire
We dance for you, O Apollon.
Lifting our baskets up high, raising flowers to the sky
We dance for you, O Apollon.

We raise our voices to the sky, a birdsong on wing to fly
We sing to you, O Apollon.
Singing to vibrant notes of light, chasing away shadows of night
We sing to you, O Apollon.

Women dancing to your lyre, like butterflies to the fire
We dance for you, O Apollon.
Lifting our baskets up high, raising flowers to the sky
We dance for you, O Apollon.

There you reach out your hand, stretching it across the land
How we adore you, O Apollon.
And you touch our face, with the warmth of your embrace
How we adore you O Apollon.

Women dancing to your lyre, like butterflies to the fire
We dance for you, O Apollon.
Lifting our baskets up high, raising flowers to the sky

We dance for you, O Apollon.

Here we dance for you, O Apollon
Here we bring a gift to you, O Apollon
Here we sing to you, O Apollon
How we adore you, O Apollon.

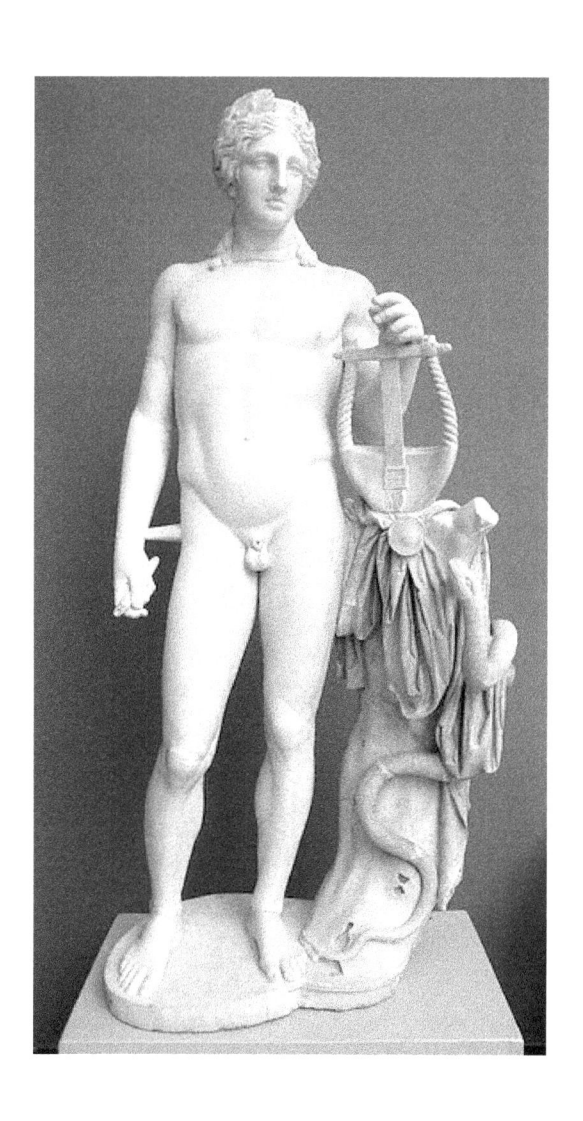

Hermes

Hermes is a silver-tongued god, the son of Zeus and Maia. He is the messenger of Zeus, and as such carries the herald's wand. He is a god who favors politics, cunning, thieves, and travelers. He is also the god who presides over contests, competitions and athletics. He became the overseer of the herds when he exchanged his lyre to Apollon for the shepherd's staff in one of his mythic pranks. Likewise, he is shepherd and guide of the souls of the dead, often working in conjunction with Hekate.

Hymn to Hermes

You God who travels all the world, every corner far-flung
Within a breath, of Zeus's will, merry god of the silver tongue
Your ennobled art brings you favor from all the gods and men
That you might kindly words to your father's ear spend
To urge his heart on this or that matter in acquiesce,
As all you have charmed since your birth and every day since
And then again you fly, deliver the case of what will be
You who travel all the space between heaven, earth and sea
Akakesios, breathe kindly upon us as you deliver his whim
Our doors are open and we welcome your good will in.

To Hermes

Hermes, how swift your feet
That ran the sacred race
That leapt the bonds
Race across the three spaces
And your mother's veil fluttered to the earth
From the day your infant legs
Stretched eagerly from her lap.
Champion of the game
You handle with such artful mastery
The polished pieces of the contest
And how agile you bend
To carry off the fruit of your victory.
How you laughed and spun the turtle shell,
Turned it about between your palms,
And death's remains became your song
Your transformation at your nimble hands
To set the seven oxen-born strings
The bold gift for Apollon,
For the twin-serpent kerykeion.
Swift herald, counselor and guide
There the numerous herds align
To the direction of your golden staff,
You carry the calf with bright hocks
Within the crook of your arm
And the wide-horned bull bellows to the cow
As they travel along the road.
Here you watch the living upon their paths
As we go and return
As each life plays the sacred game
As each runs the race toward the end
There you are, holding our hand.

To Hermes II

Where the storm brews and goads on the traveler's road
And beats continuously without lull upon the wearied brow,
Here we walk pelted with the stones of storm's night
Where the wind steals away the breath and winged terror takes flight.
Here now I am the traveler and here now I pray in absence of good day
That Hermes, swift of mind and craft,
Would lead what Apollon measured
As a shepherd before me on the path, shaking a ribboned staff
There he is laughing at the threat,
Bringing gladness and banishing dark bereft
As we draw from the shadow abode
That I may return to my golden home.

To Hermes Kharmaphron

Now, Muses, part your sweet lips to sing again,
And recall in your song the god of the curling locks,
Hermes, wanderer who delights in mischief's deeds.
Upon the road he stands, crowned with his dusty cap,
Hidden within the rolling tides of coming maiden dusk.
A mischievous sparkle alights his far-roaming eye,
And there a wicked grin curves the bow of his lip.

Honored are you Pheletes among the robber and thieves.
As a child you led away the cattle from ripe pasture,
Away from your brother's widespread golden lands.
So too do you ply your arts to assist the deceiver's game;
What lie crafts readily upon your laughing tongue,
What plot weaves together within your clever mind.
And there with slight-of-hand, Dolios, you part and separate,
A possession from the owner in fun, laughter and sport!

You laugh with the child upon your cresting hill,
Contrivers of such ingenious merriment and game.
What delight you take in their innocent machinations,
And the wild tales spun in such reckless frivolity!
Theirs are the eyes that see a world of possibility,
Sorrow and despair is not welcome to darken the view.
And in the child's hand imagination is not the gate,
Nor the path which to walk, but the opener of all things,
It rests in Hermes' hand, as their own. As the golden key.

Hail to the god of joyous pleasures and delights!
Hail to the god who contrives all impossible dreams,
To the god who would fearlessly laughs and jests
At the open mouths that would bring ruin and demise.
The shadows are kicked away by your winged foot,
It is not welcome with hanging dreary locks upon its head,
To intrude upon your well-planned games and schemes!

To Psychopompos

Limpid-eyed Muses sing now of the dark-hooded guide,
Sing of the escort of the mourned and beloved dead.
Join me in my song to honor Pyschopompos,
Heavenly son of Zeus, wanderer above and below.

There on his hill he lifts his wand, and stands the evening star,
Hearken to him the vast company of dead to follow in his tread.
There, the sons of Nyx, Hypnos and Thanotos on their nightly rounds!
Hail to you Hermes, divine leader of the souls into the hidden realm,

Welcoming into earth's embrace, leading the forth to Hades' domain.
You drive forth the spirits, as you drove forth the cattle before you,
A mantle earned from your escort of Persephone from below.
Thereafter a guide, thereafter between the worlds,
Your path is well-marked, Kerberos bows before you,
A pup at your hand, as through the darkness you lead.
The route is clear and well-traveled,
Pass the spanning Okeanos' twining stream,

Through the chambers of dreams,
And the many habitations and sacred gates,
There you lead, and lead well our dead safely in your care!

Here we pray, our message to be sent to beloved and honored dead,
Carry it away from our lips to that the world
Far beyond where Hades dwells.
Whisper our words into the phantom ear,
That they receive our love,
We shall ever remember you
And heap the offering bowl high on your holy day.
Most Honored Psychopompos,
Receive these offerings we set forth,
And hear our prayers of adoration unto you,
Who walks the trails of the dead.

Zeus

Zeus is the most supreme among the Olympians, the supreme son of Kronos and Rhea who defeated his father and took reign over the heavens and the entire world. In myth he is the father of many gods including, but not limited to, Artemis, Apollon, Ares, Hephaistos (depending on which source you ask), Hebe, Dionysos, Persephone, and Herakles. At his side is Hera, his sole counselor and wife. The power of Zeus is reflected in the lightning bolt and the shaking thunder, both deadly and awesome to mortals who have looked up into the heavens.

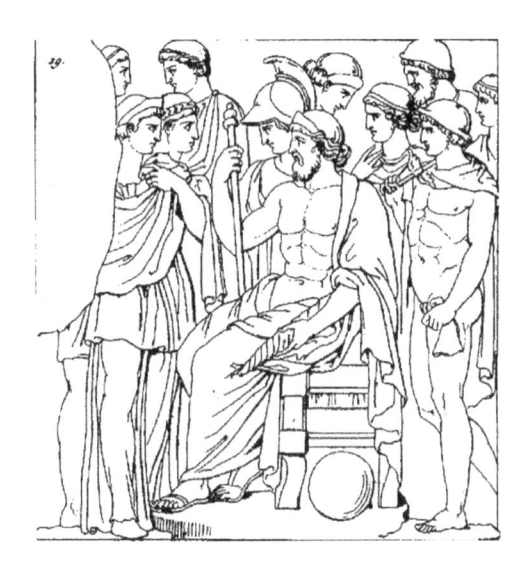

Hymn to Zeus

Eagle-eyed Zeus, far-seer, high-flier, cloud-gatherer
Far-running God, traveling all the space between the spaces
Where the ether touches there he is, beginning and end of all
Father of all, King of all, God first among the holy places
All-knowing, all-seeing, oath guardian and guest's friend
Nothing escapes you; all is delivered from you by Word and Law—
Logos, that through your bright-rayed son, to the world you send.
You are as the eagle high above, and as the lion before the sun

The bull that furrows the earth, holy seeder, at Demeter's plow
Great father of Persephone, born to go and come again
That wheat-ear child beloved by all, daughter to whom all men bow
Men and women beseech you and wait for spring's sweet return
You who gave, by creed and love, your daughter to all of the earth
As she rises and descends, this pearly bride of hidden Plouton.
Once you took her in hidden union—in a serpent's guise—
To bear of fruitful union Zagreus, cut down and torn
You wrapped about her that you were as her shell and loved
And your son makes too the yearly round, the grape-vine in the bed
Dionysos awaits his mother, before Demeter, to lift her up in the end.
Steady us on the road, be with us in our joys and travesties,
And welcome us with happy arms to that place we yearn to be.

Bull of Mykenae

Where the double doves spread their wings
And settle with their song
Upon the high lofts of ancient stone
Golden birds of light plume
Their free wings taking them on the wind
Singing in the wispy light of dawn.

From the liquid heavens comes the starry bull
He bellows and the lightning cracks

To strike the wet-sleek stone
The accepting hollow space below
Where the rain has settled dripping down
The fertile seed of heaven
To the furrows carved out of earth
By the massive curve of his golden horns.

The towering horns of kingship
Raised toward the heavenly road
A path of stars yielding to the mighty sun
The sun-point horns rising from earthly heavens
To the worlds beyond, king of his realm.
His breath is upon the ripened grain
His hooves cut the beds of great rivers
Where the spring boils from the ground.

To Zeus

The clouds break with the fierce cries, like a hunting bird in flight,
There the lightning crashes to the earth, the raindrops to the ground,
Seeds of life falling down, fingers caressing the sun-parched earth.
Zeus, dark of beard and of brow, crowned with your father's legacy,
Prayers are offered to you who bring justice among gods and men.

You stand as a mountain, a great tower shadowing in comfort all below,
The suffering man addresses to you his grievous plight.
No fraudulent oaths made beneath your scrutiny,
No guest dishonored in their stay, lawlessness takes flight
And the good hospitality of men is rewarded under your kindly might.

Hail to you of honored seat, within your counsel and the agora below
Your brow is decked in great honor, your arm enforces with strength,
And a father's affection descends to man's humble world.
Your blessings rain down fruitfully upon us from the height,
Enriching life and earth, blessing all within your emanation,

The world below stirs and rejoices, life stretches forth to your embrace.

By your will and power we shall never thirst, we shall never halt
Nor the bright headed crops grow barren upon the land,
The cool rain descends to the scarred oak, lightning-kissed
And Ge smiles propitiously upon her high-reigning son.
A hundred times we honor you, Father Zeus
 Whose tempest makes the earth tremble in onslaught,
Who drives the storms with your great aegis, unbreakable, uncontrolled,
Devouring tempest and God who sings the welcoming showers.

Hail to you Cronion, Thunderer, shaker of the vaulted heavens
Mighty hand that brushes continuously the windswept lands,
May you ever hear our pious prayers that rise to you
From every temple, from our hearts, and our humble hearths below.

Zeus of Olympos

There is a great tower bridging earth, heaven and bright sky,
And the breadth that does expand to every corner of time,
Where there that gods do dwell touching present and history past.
There Zeus reigns crowned upon his father's throne,
Great Olympos, divine rulership of all space and all time.
Where is a place that his hand does not extend?
What day comes by that within all things he does not exist?

Zeus walks with great footsteps across the lands,
As a welcome guest that we would not suspect,
Whether feathered majestic bird floating to the ground,
Or the branches stretching far of an ancient oak standing proud,
He may join in accompaniment to the river's laughing song,
Or be the cry of thunder upon the autumn winds.
Among all things Zeus does walk, and all life bears his fingerprint,
Fashioned with loving hands and filled with a spark of divine breath,
A bit of him is there in everything that breathes and lives.

And within the holy temple grounds, where his children find their rule,
All in accordance all in reverence to their father's will.
Athene proudly declares and defends her father's sacred law,
Loxias from his sacred lands uttering his father's right word.
Within their temple grounds there he is present still.
Time and history within his grasp
From when he knocked his father down,
And caged Time within his rule, and set the order of the universe.
The Horae bow to him, in their brightly colored veils, for their part
In the dance that was orchestrated and conducted by most holy Zeus.

The stars give due reverence in the orbit of their paths that he did set,
Their travel through the heavens' night
Telling of the passage of the road of time.
Nowhere does his hand not present,

Nowhere left untouched by his foot,
And his seed in humanity forever germinates one generation into next.
That spark of divine, from Zagreas his infant son, kindled in our hearts,
From the aged past down to the little newly born in the flush of youth.
Present within us, present all around us,
Tall tower standing behind our gods,
All reverence and love due to you most holy Zeus, king of all the world.

The Child Zeus

Upon the ancient mountain heights, timely weather-worn,
Secreted to a hidden cave from the earthen womb he was born,
Rhea groaned with the shaking earth to deliver her youngest babe.
The rain pelted down with lightning flash, moisture to fruitful earth,
Bearing forth a regal brow among nymphs of mountain heights.
Heaven-born, earthly-born, a mighty child nursed with tender love,
Spring bees hastened with their laden boughs of honey to his lips,
And parched with libations of milk from the moon-kissed nymphs.
Helios shone brightly down, brightened the skies for reckless child play,
And Selene lulled him in her soft glow,
Night birds singing him sweetly to sleep.
And upon the holy mountain slopes,
A growing youth raised song and dance,
Among the trailing company of celebration in his rites
Followed the nurse nymphs.
Loud-shaking shouts and songs trembled
From mountain rise to sweeping shores,
Heavens and earth thundered at his dance
Echoing across worlds and lands.
To touch all things from his dance and holy song,
Uplifted voice of a son's devoted love,
Risen high and loud, with bountiful libations
Pouring forth, to the queenly mother Rhea.
He celebrates her shaking steps as she strides across the lands,
He lifts his voice to sing the howling winds

Drifting from her locks' coiling strands.
A great queen who reaches heaven's heights,
As a mountain juts from its rocky bed,
Terrible and great, most powerful queen
Celebrated and beloved by revered son.
Over the mountains he darts,
As a young lion boasting the breadth of his flaming mane,
Shaking the earth and azure skies with the mighty roar of his wild cry.
Born in power for a great fate
That has been woven on the loom's immortal web,
Limitless power, touching all life,
Mighty to challenge his father's crown,
To raise up from the mountain's ground,
Bringing order and law to his throne.
By his might, savage might,
Born and risen on the mountain's tempest side,
To his hand order ties all things bound,
Pride of his deep-girdled mother Rhea.

Demeter

     Demeter is daughter of Kronos and Rhea, and mother of Persephone by Zeus. At times she has also been called the mother of Dionysos and of Artemis. Demeter is a torch-bearing goddess of the wheat and poppy flowers. She is the queen of the Mysteries at her holy place in Eleusis. She overtakes her mother's role as mighty goddess of the earth. Yearly she grieves for the absence of her daughter and winter falls over the earth. Every spring trees bud and flowers bloom and young shoots of wheat rise as she rejoices the return of her child.

Hymn to Demeter
Demeter, tender of the young green shoots of spring,
Seed-bringer, grand cultivator to you our prayers we send.
Fragrant-crowned, you walk the rows with torch in hand,
You, who received Zeus the planter in your fertile bed.
Harvest yielder to bind and thresh the autumn wheat,
Their golden heads submit with joy at the circle's end.

Sun-crowned goddess who rules the small garden gate,
Anesidora the gracious you open your kindly hand.
Poppy-loving lady, to you our supplicating arms uplift,
To you, O Chthonia, ruler of the four corners of the land.
For you, on eagle's wings the sphinx in haunting tune sings
Fair Deo, you whose perfumed arms over the world span.

Mother of Kore, guardian of the gate, bright mother of all,
We hail you upon the curving road, we follow your light.
Receiver of Poseidon who holds in his arms the radiant shore,
Bend your head, Antaea, receive our prayers kindly in your sight.
As we walk unwavering on the road carved by Persephone
We praise you great Brimo, goddess of unconquerable might!

To Demeter

Muses dancing among the Graces, celebrating earth's gifts to men,
Dance and sing with me now in honor of corn-crowned Demeter.
Ruddy-faced Demeter, mantled in the colors of the earth,
She sits upon her drakon cart, the swineherds' feast lain before her.
All honor to You, Sito! By your pleasure we shall not be want of bread,
From your hand, flower-faced Chloe,
The poppy spreads its children to the land.

From your brother's embrace,
Your blossom child did come to life and arise,
As a seed sown in the soil, rises forth to rain and sun,
So did Persephone rise with a blossom face,
Cherished daughter beloved.
What delight did come to your mother's heart
To spy your daughter so fair,
Paint the petals with delicate handicraft in maiden's company,
Entrusted to the attendance of goddesses virtue pure,
To dance in a meadow sunlit.

O Demeter, our hearts grieve with you
When your daughter departs the living earth,
See now the torn hair and streaming tears that are shed!
But still we set to you a bountiful feast, and delight to ease your heart,
And we plant the winter seed to the promise of the renewing spring.
Even as winter holds us in its grasp of ice and snow,
We come together there before the tended roaring fires,
And into our family fold invite you, sorrowing,
Into the warmth of home.

Behold spring rising again, the earth prepares for the return of Kore,
From the dark castle of her beloved husband in the other world.
Happy is your heart, to see the brightening glow of the yew torch,
Hekate's leading the procession, and lo Persephone arises!

Happy are our hearts to greet the blushing spring maiden, Deione;
Where her slim feet touch the earth, there life stirs and springs anew,
And before her fair form we sing praises to you, great bountiful mother.

To Demeter II

Summer winds to the end, greeting autumn winds and rains,
And there Demeter is enthroned,
Crowned with acorns and russet leaves,
Woven firmly with the yellow pearly heads of the harvest grains.
In her hand is a horn, a bread-basket spilling forth,
And the tender autumnal fruits
Spilling as blessing across the ground.

Bright-eyed, flushed-cheeked and rosy-lipped,
Demeter holds the plow,
To sow winter seeds to wait out in slumber
Until dawning spring,

Autumn comes a time of labor
By the sweat of men's sunlit brow.
Bright blush of color streaks across the land,
A final song before winter rest,
A musky scent of ripened earth
Rises across the sweeping winds.

The sun sinks quickly down, a descent that lengthens
The winter coming night,
And a song rises to the skies of summer birds
Starting the southern flight.
Pale goose feathers are woven in her hair,
Flying on breezes across the earth,
And late summer-ripe berries stain the curve of her mouth
And potent on her tongue,
Wine-dark grapes hang like a precious gem,
A sweet gift from the vineyard son.

There she stands under the wind-shaken boughs,
Where the acorn and almond falls,
O sweet and bitter, tender fruits of the earth,
Blessed gift to feed the children,
To keep the races of beast and man
Until the hard blight of winter's end.

Hail to Demeter who bears the great curving horn of plentitude,
Upon our lips are the praises of the earth-reigning mother,
Corn-bearing queen,
Earth-gowned goddess, draped in yellow,
Draped in russet and draped in green,
May harvest be great, winter be mild, and in due time
Hasten the return of maiden spring!

To Demeter III

The Muses sing of a season turned,
Their voices carried upon the brisk flirting wind,
Whose breath is a laughing breeze
That strives to unravel the maidens' modesty.
Beneath his onslaught bright-eyed Phthinophoron happily shrieks,
Autumn gathers about the earth her finest veil,
Adorn with its gold and scarlet thread.
Her moist breath is a vapor upon the land,
A mist that hides away the grief in the morn.
And wherever that she may touch with her golden hand
Brightens to the autumnal hue,
Drawing up the wealth of the worlds
And laying them before Demeter's golden feet.

The trees are like a living flame,
Bending down their boughs of russet and gold,
And the sap is a rich honey
That runs as a musky river to the deep-furrowed ground.
The world lies within its final flush of life
Before the season of slumberous rest,
Gilded expertly in the shades of precious metals
That rest beneath the holy ground.
All of life dying so sweetly, so beautifully,
A blessed nurture for the generations of the earth,
Where the mighty trees bow their weighted heads
And the flower loosens its petals to the wind.

The heavens shake with the thunderous rain,
And where it kisses the receiving ground,
The fruits of the earth do greatly swell
Brimming with the promise of fertile life,
Falling from her horn, the earth does yield
In plenty what the harvest brings.

See there where Demeter is enthroned,
Upon a seat of living stone,
Clothed in the fire of the earth,
The thousand hues of yellow, russet, orange and gold,
A bright tapestry draped across her knees
Detailing in art the laborious joys of autumn.
Her eyes are like that of a doe,
Her cheeks are stained with a ruddy glow,
Illuminated by the weeping streams that flow
From her heart to the dusty ground.

The fall of her hair is the ripened wheat,
Rippling like the waves of a placid sea,
There Demeter wears her crown,
Twined as a briar upon her brow, a tangle of fruit and leaf.
It is like the dying sun that sinks the west,
Upon her head a brilliantly colored crest,
And at breast she is adorned with bright jewels
Of dragonflies and fairest beauty of butterflies,
They are as a ringlet around her neck,
Adorning life's fragility sculpted carefully upon their wings.
Little spirits blown about on the winds,
Released from that earthbound gown without a home,
And there they rest on her breast
In their brightest color to await their descent,
Down to the dead where the winged ones
Upon death's banks in their colored robes gather.

At her feet twines gnarled roots, of ancient seasons past;
And the dusky dragon rests, his eye like a cavern jewel,
Guarding the earth's great wealth, the serpent at the hearth.
He guards not precious stones, nor lumps of ore and gold,
But rather a treasure sealed, bonded with blood to the land,
Shared within the heart, of familial ties and loyalty.

Guard the table of the family, safeguard the erect house standing tall,
Thunderous one rest silently,
Deter famine and secure Demeter's ripened crop,
To nurse and nurture the family,
Forging the loving bonds and generations to come.
We set the plate for Demeter,
Welcome her with feast and happy song,
And of the wine from the ripened vine,
Pour a heavy sweet libation upon the ground,
The sweetest fragrant nectar enjoyed by men,
Draining into her grey stone cup.

Before her all life celebrates a respite
Before the slow walking season of night,
The birds are as a flag boasting the many hues of the land,
As they wing through heaven;
And the flocks take flight,
To soar above the portrait of the land following the journey of the sun.
The beasts of the wood and field join among the merry feasts,
Before they close their eyes,
Before they find their long rest
Within the embrace of deadly winter's sleep.
And there just beyond, upon a not-too-distant hill,
Artemis prepares and sets her string,
Awaiting to receive season's monthly turn
And rule the land by her golden horn bow!

Hail to Demeter, the kindly mother,
Raising men by your bounty and bringing them to greater things,
Hail to you in the dying season,
Bringer of all things to ripe maturity of harvest for their flesh;
And you plant the infant seed within the womb of the ground
To return with maiden spring,
By which to forever nurture
The earthly races of great beasts and those of man.

Winter Song to Demeter

Silence is a draping veil, a melody of icy webs within its wintry frost,
A breath of clarity, and the chords of purity, woven on the breeze.
The ground is barren, dormant, quiet: a death sigh all around
To echo the keening cries of a mother forlorn, a mother grief-torn.
Ice it shudders on its perch, a crash of tiny bells as it falls,
Torn away by the wails vibrating currents in the loud quiet.
Season of night casts her shadow against the brief hours of day,
And gowns all things in shades of grieving grey that the mother brings.
Demeter, her heart chilled with somber tears: seeking, yearning,
Painting pale hues across her face of snow and barren stone.
What darkness she wears as her veil, night spun fabric all around,
And crowned upon her brow, the skeletal fingers of vegetation sleeping
Encased within the ice of frozen dew, running down into her hair,
Tangled burnished threads, held glacially, matted with frost and ash.
Not a single joyous sound, the winter birds have far fled her step
The bony fingers of brush and trees tap an eerie staccato beat
Where they touch like moans shaken from the ground.
In grievous search of Persephone, and even the sun he pulls away
That the fair girl of blossom face has gone to rest in Hades' embrace,
There Demeter wanders with pale light, flickering torch in the night,
All life, beast and man join in her weeping,
And the earth quietly sleeping.

II
The Daughter And The Son

Hymns To Persephone And Dionysos

This section praises and calls to the Gods of the Mysteries, Persephone and Dionysos. The basic role of these gods deals directly with the life cycle of mankind leading from life, to death, and to life again. In this manner these are the gods closest and most beloved of humanity. These are the gods that are walking beside us, and their stories are the stories of ourselves. There are several festivals through the year that honor these gods in which this hymns would be appropriate or any personal prayer that you may wish to offer these words would do.

Persephone

Persephone is the daughter of Demeter and Zeus, whose mythic retreat to the land of her husband Hades to spend part of the year is probably the best known of the myths as we observe the yearly cycle between spring and fall. She was also the mother of Zagreus, by Zeus when he mated with her in the form of a serpent, who was captured and torn apart by Titans. She is also connected to Adonis whom she shared with Aphrodite in a cyclic similar to Persephone's own yearly appearance and departure.

Persephone

Autumn seed buried within the earth,
Born from the flesh of the mother,
Born from the liquid rain of the father.
Safely kept within the heart of the earth,
A palace of riches unseen and unknown.
Only the children, the dead, can see,
The things buried deep from mortal eyes,
And there she waits, within those hollowed walls,
Dwelling in the land of dormant sleep.

She is daughter of the earth and married to wealth,
A child bride, a kernel planted deep below,
Into the earth the tender fruitful seed was sown.
Demeter's children descend to death and arise,
Following Persephone's path and the son divine.
The daughter seed, bred by flower kissed from heaven,
And the flower matures to fruit and bears within her womb,
Sweet seed of spring, seed of life, to be sown within the ground.

Spring sun invites the earth, to release her bounty,
The dead rejoiced in living offering and prayers,
Delivered by Hermes, the messenger below.

Psychopompos descended, into the earth, to the dead,
Then by the double-yew-light to the living they led.
Persephone arises, tender shoot from ripened seed,
Flowery footsteps across the earth, spring she does lead.

Happy is the mother, Happy is the daughter,
Happy in garland, and crowned is Zeus' returning son,
The earth breathes the cool sigh of a winter's end,
And in the horizon the increased hours of Helios' golden descent.
Happy Spring, Persephone returned,
Sweet limited time, and then to sink to earth again,
Bride of Hades, fosterer of the loving shadow dead.

Persephone, Hades' Queen

O shadowed Persephone, walking through Hades' hall,
Stately bride of Plouton,
Upon your head is a twisted crown of vines and winter violets
And that pale luminance of your cheek,
How like the glow of the hanging moon
Shining so soft in death's abode where the heavenly light is unseen.
Merciful are your arms that embrace the dead
Who travel the road you have taken,
You who are child and lover,
Hold at your breast the wearied dead in their rest
As you once held born of your womb and Zeus the father, Zagreus,
Infant souls of the flame that dispersed by his flesh:
Those fragile children – humanity.
There you dwell and reign, candle in the dark,
Dancing in the halls of the dead
The warm breath that billows in gentle caress
Upon your husband's brow
With wide night-mantled arms
To lovingly give of your heavenly embrace.
O divine light so sweetly perfumed
By spring and summer the living seasons,
Sitting upon an golden throne,
Beloved of Hades, bright-veiled Persephone.

The Road of Persephone

Little girl, Persephone
Born among the fragrant buds
Where each petal has crystal drops
Of heaven's moist dew.
Her cradle was the flower beds
And the even furrows
Where new grain shined green
Newborn heads tilted to the sun.

She too tilted her gaze to the light
And clung to her mother
To her golden rows of hair
In the comfort of her dawn
In the tender blossom of her youth.

The first flowers of spring
The sprinkling of the summer seed
Her womb swelled great
With the planting from Zeus' rape
Where the serpent descended slow
Into the hollow of her mother's stone.
He coiled all about and she obeyed
To open the chaste rock of ground
To the falling rain of heaven's own.
The mixed substances bore its fruit
To bear her first sacred course
Zagreus springing from the furrow
From his mother's gentle house.

In the summer she had danced
She laughed and sang the swallow's song
Out of the reach of the cooing doves
In the garden of the world
Each flower bowing to the sun.
And every flower's gown
Owed is prestige to her hand
Her painted love, tears and memories
Upon the vessels of her land.
Persephone danced her bright road
Upon the ruby poppy field
Beneath Athena's bright veil
Beside the contest of Artemis.

Her unchanging road of summer
Closed its quiet eyes
When Eros drew his bow taunt
And let the golden arrow fly.
Her haunting grief's lament
At the death of Zagreus
Shorn into seven parts divided
Echoed in the sway of her dance
Moving farther from the golden garden.
In the far reaches where she played
The earth twisted in display
A new road opened upon itself
And a willful grasp carried her away.

Persephone is on the road of stone
Where death lays upon the field
And the thousand seeds fly
To scatter on the ground
Where sad-eyed souls whisper
Close to the earth for their days.
There Plouton with his crystal crown
Seats her upon an emerald throne,
The quiet wealth of stone
That knows neither joy nor life,
Holding the court of earthly joy and sorrow.
His will keeps her on the road
There Persephone is the queen.

Where is the waiting spring?
Where is the Kore dressed in green?
She is coming, quietly coming...
By Zeus' rule she returns
Upon the small road ever waiting
With two bright lights leading

Leading to Demeter's garden.
Dionysos smiles there at the end
Where the poppies raise their heads
Holding aloft for her the ivy wreath
And the vine for her to receive
The stock held at fruitful ready
To gather to her a new gown of divinity.

Persephone

Khaire Persephone, extinguisher of torches,
Killer of the flame, you snuff out the light.
You moon-faced goddess, blessed daughter
Of Demeter, wrapped in the wintry veil of night.
You, first beyond the small garden gates,
Brightest flower of dewy golden petals,
There you graciously descend to rise again,

Goddess twice-crowned in the golden metals.
As the tree drops her rich summer's leaves
In quiet slumber, in her deep winter sleep
So too do you drop your bright robe of gold
To become the grain of wheat, the sown seed
That you may rise up again to bear the fruit
Held in the wide embrace of royal Bakkhos,
You blessed child of Demeter and Zeus.

Persephone II

Gentle Kore, you walk with soft sunlight in your hair,
You sweet tulip maiden, your perfumed skirts
Like the petals of spring flowers, waft at your ankles
And the pale daffodils drip sweet nectar upon your toes
As the blooms of hyacinth drift heady musk to the sun;
But none comparable to the sweet bud of your face
You blossomed from the egg, your twelve petals unfold
Shining flower of your mother's high-walled garden
Sewn by the love of Zeus, you come again and we greet you
Hail to you, Persephone, goddess regal and bright-veiled!

Dionysos

 The son of Zeus and Semele, Dionysos was prematurely born when his mother died from exposure to the full glory of Zeus. Hermes rescued Dionysos who was afterward sewn into the thigh of his father to continue to grow to term. Myth connects him also to Zagreus, the son of Zeus and Persephone, as he was reborn from the remaining heart. Dionysos journeyed to many places, including to Anatolia, in order to cure his madness brought onto him by Hera. There he was also, according to myth, taught the mysteries to bring to the world. Dionysos is god of cultivation and wine, the god wielding the thyrsus and accompanied by maenads and satyrs. As such he is considered a reveling god and a god of the theater, as he stands at the pinnacle of mankind's joys and sorrows.

Dionysos

Proud stalk that rises from your father's loins
The rain that issues from the thunder cloud
The sleek showers sowing the fertile ground
Where sweet water gushes upon silent rocks
And the world thrives, ripe with new life.
You hold the potent cup to our lips
 A heady fluid we cannot grasp
A sip—
A taste—
A river of life moving within us
An ecstasy without drug
 Only but of your love
  And a promise given.

To Dionysos

Fair-voiced daughters of Zeus,
You turn your gaze and lift your song,
For among you the bright-haired Graces
And doe-eyed nymphs do rejoice,
That there in the slumbering woods,
Rouses Dionysos with his clamorous band.
His lips curve wide a mocking smile
And his eyes flash illumination in the dark,
He is the cat wearing the sly grin,
As he stalks among the women dancing.
Hail bull-voiced Dionysos!
Hail devouring night-maned lion!

Beloved son of Zeus and Semele,
Beloved in the care of sweet-lipped nymphs,
Beloved by all to whom you turn
Your lusty bright gaze in the hidden night.
And they beloved to you
Who receive you with welcoming fair arms,
To them your gifts splash down,
A wild running stream, and pour forth!

Frenzied voices rise, maenadic dance
To greet the bright-eyed god,
Donning the leopard skin,
And astride the spotted flank and back,
Into their loud-voiced company you enter
Upon the wild screaming cat.
But the leopard does not turn claws
To the jubilant rushing crowd,
Stayed under Bacchic hand
Is your dancing golden mount.
The earth and seas shake before your wide-treading steps,

Shivering in delight,
Welcoming to receive the blessed seed of the vine
Within its rich breast.
The vine is a merciless tangle,
Stretching delicate fingers thirsting to the sky,
It fills the cup sweet with life,
But too much and death is the cup that men partake.
There you pluck it up for your twining wreath
And flowered crown, to set upon thy head.

To Dionysos the Bull

Muses sing of the night nymph's clatter and maenad wild dance,
Sing of ivy-crowned Dionysos, night-wandering, far-shouting god.
His graceful arms and bright brow are wreathed among ivy and vine,
And there he rises from his companion loud-crying midst,
As a bull rising from a windswept violent sea beyond the shore.

Hail Dionysos, a prayer to you falls wild from my parted lips!
You shake those dark locks of hair, the earth shudders and rolls,
As the mighty bull, to clear the dust, would shake his vibrant hide.
Violently you tear and feast, your cup brims never to empty,
And that liquid of life spills upon the earth, a holy seed planted within.

The maenads drink that cup, heifers readying before the roaring bull,
Rejoicing, embracing, and kissing that dark-bearded jaw.
Bull-horned god, horns crowned as crescents upon your immortal brow,
Where you walk and rest plenty reigns, fruits blossom from seed.
To you we praise for the virile seed, for the life that springs and renews.

To Dionysos II

Dark night hides things well,
All are shadows moving beneath her veil,
Darkest night, great equalizer of men,
We who travel in the unknown,
In acceptance or with fear upon our breath.

The darkness wraps all around, diminishing the strong,
Mighty have fallen to the terrors of the hidden things.
Dionysos runs and leaps through the darkest hours,
With his maenads in company over mountains they bound,
Raising cry upon the wind, Dionysos of the night cries,
That brings great men shuddering in their keep.

Darkness closes our eyes and takes us back to beginning times,
Before we knew the birth-greeting of the light of day.

Brave men shudder in terror of a second womb – the earth a tomb,
And we descend into the unknown upon the winding paths.
Meager torches light but a small space,
So our feet to not tarry or trip along the way.
Lo there in the distance is the thyrsus burning bright,
The flames dancing upon Dionysos' holy stalk, a torch.

He lights the way to the unknown, illuminator of the night,
To the depths he leads, away from civilization's towering walls,
To the mysteries of the queen, fruit-giving mother earth.
Night noises, night songs, terror-riding things,
Like spotted cats shrieking in delight – falling upon their prey;
Terrible and great all at once, kindly and deathly at the same,
Are those gods – the trembling Earth and Evacos who holds the vine.

Good friend to men, walking in company at his side,
To descend to ground, to see themselves in truth – in flaming light.
Dionysos pulls away our masks, his wine inflames within,
There it lurks exposed, the true nature and character of men.
Bare and true as babes newborn to enter into Earth's tender fold.
As sweet wine paves the way in libations poured,
Dionysos leads the way to the sacred chamber, the shadowed room.

Let us rejoice when we truly see, the way the cycle turns,
Where lives of men are dust in time, the wheel ever spinning.
From a mother's flesh we rise and to a mother's we again descend,
Sweet spring of youth fades eventually to winter's grace,
And we come to sing in the lands of the earth's child dead.
Persephone leads the way, she greets us at the gates,
Into her hold, into her embrace, a cycle never ends,
From her kingdom we shall shine and arise a flower born.

Iakhos leads a wine-sweet sleep, small death from which all awake
And there he leads the flowing streams, of libations to their ends.

Into our ears it is he that speaks of sacred things,
Dionysos lights the way, Dionysos is the road,
And he leads all ways to all things small and great.
Here leads this holy road, and crowns us on our path,
To bring us to a most worthy destination at its end.

Into earth he descends for the cherished dead,
Leading them to the place that waits, receiving libations so lovingly.
Speaking of the things known in the heart of earth – that unquiet cave,
The winter flame burning bright within the hollowed temple of Delphi.
And gentle spring sun greets him well; the vine rises from the furrow,
There his gift replenishes in fruitful mass for another season's turn,
As Dionysos dances in great leaps across the blossomed earth.

The Son

O wind of a thousand voices sing to me
Upon a leaf, upon nature's hollows, or rustic reed
Through the labyrinth of time winds the melody
Singing in breezy breath of a place beyond memory.
There a child, panther-gowned, feasted on milk and honey
Nurtured at breasts of bronze-faced nymphs
Amid a fragrant blossom-bed, dripping nectar to his lips.
There the violet-wreathed nymphs would shake their locks
With hands upraised gracefully they dance and sing
Circling about the boy of their bower as butterflies to a flower.
Upon his head they set a crown of woven leaves
And he took his first sips of first passion's innocence
From the deep wells of their perfumed lips.
Limitless was the terrain where his foot did step
Boundless was the scope of the wild dance
Across the earth his gifts spilled from golden hands.
Child born of heaven's power, heir of heaven's reign.

III
The Titans
And Primordial Gods

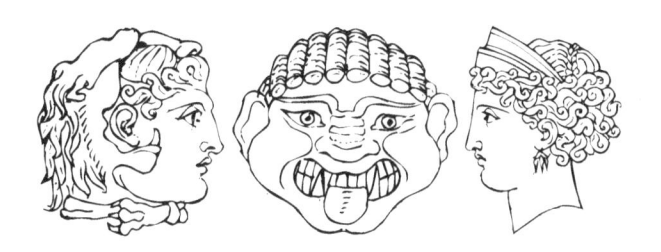

Though perhaps less often on the receiving end of our prayers and devotions comparable to other deities, these ancient primordial gods and Titans do from time to time receive their due recognition. Perhaps it is the sun as the seasons change themselves over with the revolving equinoxes and solstices. Perhaps it is the earth as spring renews and autumn bears fruit; or it may be the moon on her monthly course, pulling at the tides of the ocean that we might wish to honor and libate to in our rituals and prayers. Whatever the occasion may be, there are times when we wish to honor the innate spirits of the world around us, and these hymns presenting in this section are devoted to just that purpose.

Nyx

Primordial night, mother of all beginnings; she is the mother of Gaia and Ouranos, who in turn parents the Titans that eventually parent the gods. As such she is the progenitor of all creation that is born from her.

Nyx
Dusky night I sing to you, haunted voice, great and wide-spanning,
You who mothered thousands; you who witnessed creation's dawn.
Hail to you mother night, the world is your infant asleep in your arms,
As your luminous-eyed messengers whisper in our dreaming ears;
Here your voice is the crooning melody of a hundred night-loving frogs,
Your song is the haunting harmony
Of all creatures born awakened to the night.

Your arms are fragrant as the night-blossoms
Opening wide to the moon,
And your perfumed skin is dusted with a drowsy powder
That falls on all beneath you,
From where you rise, across the sky,
From the dark stallion mount your skirts fan wide,
Billowing, rolling darkness where ends rest and beginnings born.
There the moon is like your bright face,
A shining orb of sweet countenance,
And the stars are threads of silver,
Little jewels woven in the night of your hair,
That they rest scattered over your arms, waist and brow
Floating through the heavens.

Lo, there I see the sun has sank beyond the horizon crest,
The last beams of light catching hold
Of the tendrils of your wildly flying hair.
Owl-eyed Nyx riding the skies,

Your breath fans night moisture into the air,
And where your twilight thighs clasp
The sides of your long-maned mount,
His flesh quivers, leaping into air,
Midnight galloping across the sky.
Night thunder and rains shake the skies
From the heavy brush of his hooves,
Lightning of night within his eyes,
Wild mount for you, my lady Nyx.

On the land where you arise, the child breathes a gusty sigh,
Milky cheeks flushed with sleep, resting so sweetly beneath your kiss.
And there before you spy the lovers entwined where Eros happily plays,
You drape them gently within the velvet night,
Hidden secure from daylight's sight.
Hidden are all things within the dark of your robe,
Not to be banished by sweet light of night,
There the shadows beneath the light play upon the canvas of the world,
So that all the night comes to life, hiding the real, revealing the fantasy,
For what may lurk that we cannot see
Within the voluminous folds of your mighty robe.

Dark-browed Nyx, you are of a frightening form
To give evil a terror of night,
And then you are so kindly-faced
Like a mother with a babe in her care,
Most awesome and wide-armed,
You hold the bridles of the mighty teams,
To loosen the nightmares, they thunder across the world,
Shaking the silk of their manes.
But in your other hand a hundred more
Of sweet-tempered mares, bright-eyed,
Loosen them in great numbers
To bring sweetest dreams to your slumbering child.

Sender of terrors, merciful mother,
All of the living submits to your holy power,
For night is a power limitless,
Closing your unwearied eyes only at the rising of day.

The Creation

Muses sing your fair song, kindled forth in the torches of life,
Illuminate the halls of memory to sing of the beginning times.
In the beginnings of beginnings, born before all of time,
Vast and formless Nyx, crowned in primal ice,
Held aloft the little diamond in her night; held Ge to her breast.
Silent stone, beautiful sphere settled in her place of purity,
Virgin egg held safe and fast within the motherly arms.

But there Ge finally sighed, a breathe of wind,
Weight of density drew her more compact,
Forming the diamond, hardening the ore,
Drawing in the solid weight of stone to her core.
Such a strife that broke away from the arms of mother Night,
And there the tears filled the abyss, there Nyx wept.
The fall of her tears gathered to bear the sea of heaven,
Wrapping Ge in his damp embrace, Ouranos lain over earth.

There in that cosmic sea, in the oceans of heaven,
Ge laughed and pulsed in a dance upon his tide.
There she swam through his embrace,
And lines of merriment creased her lovely face,
Maturing and gaining dimension was most beautiful Ge.
The hills of the breast swelled, and the valley ran deep,
To where the hidden caves opened their wide mouths.

Perfume-breathed Eros joined between them,
Attracted the union, flamed the passion, of Ouranos to bed with Ge,
Upon the bed of love he took her, under the blanket of Night.

The ether crept and caressed, in the canyon, in the cave,
It penetrated past the stony mantle to ignite resting fire.
The ethers joined within the belly of wide-flanked earth,
And her womb trembled with the life, and water born,
Loud speaking Okeanos rushing from his mother's arms,
And draws his sister Tethys, the nurturing, to his hearth,
Where they Eros united to bear the rivers of the earth.

Ge, mother of mothers, bore many babes in the heavenly embrace,
Bore many children to the sea that surrounded her so well,
And from her were born the many species, the many nations,
All those things that live under the light, Hyperion her son,
Who in turn bedded Theia, seeing all, fathered the bright-rayed sun.
All the Titans sprung from first generation born from the earth,
Delivered and received in Ge's maternal arms, in her love,
And so Rhea was born, favored and daughter most beloved.
Violent Kronos too was their son, who would shed his father's blood,
But fall to his own son, hidden in Ge's abodes,
For the rise of Olympians.

Ge/Gaia

The earth, also known as Ge or Gaia is the spirit of our planet and substance of earth. She is a part of every stone, every tropical paradise, every desert, grassland, bog and forest. She is a part of the concrete part of us all, down to the atoms of life there she is, and we are a part of her as are all living forms and all species, and all inanimate forms. If Nyx is the mother of all, then Ge is the mother of all this planet and all things contained within it.

To the Earth
Mother, first mother
Mother we sing to you.
From your body we were born
And sheltered within your embrace.
Kind mother who protects and shields,
And we were too in our tender infancy.
We dwelt within the ground
Blind to the world, O fearsome world.
But we left your hollowed flesh
Never forgetting Mother's gifts.
Medicine springs forth,
Sustenance springs forth,
Great waters spring forth,
All is a river flowing with plenty.
You give without request,
And receive us with welcoming arms.
For we return to you again when life ends,
To dwell within, that land which welcomes our spirits.
You harbor our ancestors in the deep land,
And there we shall see and greet them again.
You, mantled Mother,
To You we sing.

Kronos

    Kronos, king of the world who, against the wishes of Ge married Rhea, but devoured his children Hades, Poseidon, Demeter, Hestia and Hera that they might not usurp his throne as he had done to his father. However, his youngest child was not eaten but hidden away from him with Ge. Zeus eventually overtook Kronos and released his siblings and won the throne of heaven. Kronos was the god of the Golden Age, an age where nothing aged and all was plentiful. His defeat put the cosmos in order and regulated life.

To Kronos

O bittersweet time, windswept and ages born,
Never to touch immortal brow or the Muses fair.
In the distance you hear a sigh, a song, carried far,
Soft lips open to sing of passing ages, settled dust,
Lost in fabrics of time that history pass and legend rise.
You are the great concealer that blurs mortal mind,
As the glass tumbles, there the sands sift and depart.

Devastating Kronos, you weather the fair cheek and limb,
And the mortals before you do both rejoice and despair.
To welcome grievous memories dimmed in your passage,
To touch the comb to the aging locks, color has faded and gone.

Destroyer Kronos, you who are both merciful and unkind,
Hear our prayers that your passage does not like a viper strike.
Take not our wit, clever thought or memory of great deed,
And with great grace lay upon the aging face a gentle hand.

Though the gods do not quell before you and do not yield,
For you cannot strip away that golden immortal crown,
Still they measure the mortal days that subsides to you.
Selene gathers to her the lights of night, brightest shining one,
And proud son of Hyperion lights the darkened sky at dawn.
Immortal gods stir within that dome the heavenly dance,
The tread of Hekate, Hera the guide, and starry-bannered Zeus,
Time's dance the stars spin above the earth in a dance so grand.

Tell to us great Kronos, memory-keeper of those forgotten songs
From where all beginning had begun, repeats its heavenly ballad.
Heaven and Earth still embrace, and a season goes around,
Wither life, fall to death and decay, forgotten to all and then reborn!
Kronos you view the turning from your castle, from you golden shore,
Offer your regard and embrace to the fleeting life you graze,
And greet to you the perfumed dead to your kingdom, to your home.

Tethys

The mother of all forms of fresh water on earth; the rivers, the wells and springs are her children. She is the wife of Okeanos, from whose name we get the English word ocean. She also served as a foster mother to Hera.

To Tethys

Primordial one, crowned upon the earth and heavens,
By union of Ge and Ouranos you were conceived and born,
Like a dewy shower upon the earth yielding ripest fruits.
To the rushing water you were taken as a youthful bride,
To dwell with Okeanos in a castle at Earth's edge,
Where Eileithyia tended to your labor cries of many children born.

By your hand and art you learned to draw from the running water,
To draw up the fountain from the body of your sleepless spouse,
And there within your belly, water mingled with your fertile ground,
Bearing fruit within of many daughters and many sons,
Drawing up the fountain to nurture their quick-running forms.

Of greatest mothers are you, your womb so great,
From the fruitful cavern all rivers of the earth rushed out,
Strong rushing sons, and lovely daughters with flowing hair,
To wind into the deepest houses within the earth,
To rise up into roaring rivers, gentle springs and laughing streams.
Lusty sons and nurturing daughters who kindly tend to little babes.

And gauzy dewdrop Nephelai were too from her body born,
Taking swiftest winged course to the embrace of air.
Moisture-bearing, fruitful daughters, nurturing and replenishing,
Receiving the waters of brothers and sisters and releasing it down again.
Little nurses, fair-haired and soft-eyed, dancing within the sky.

So great is your flowing nurture, nurse of so many young,
That to your arms Hera was delivered, stately daughter of Rhea.
Little fosterling daughter, nursed under your most tender care,
Raised in happy youth in your most regal house.
To her lightning-quick clever mind, you passed along your arts,
By her hand she drew forth the nurturing waters to the earth
That she should be protector and succor those in her care,
Destined in to be great Queen among gods and men.

Hail to you Tethys, regally born, regally bred, rich in life,
Nurse of many, mother of many, daughter of the Earth.

Eros

Eros is a bit tricky to place because he is the primordial force of love and eventually became the son of Aphrodite and Ares, and married Psyche, a reflection of the soul. In myth he is said to possess two arrows, one golden one that brought love, and a lead one that brings the opposing emotion when struck by it.

To Eros

Little ancient, beloved of blushing Muses, faces stained in adoration
Each in turn singing passion's praises in alteration,
To the primal laughing-eyed who flies in sweet disguise.
With feathered wings, downy plumes, on every wind alighting,
Where the ether touches and twines, there he rides
Whether on spring's breaths or autumn's billows,
Among the heady summer bliss or winter's frigid kiss;
Entwining earth to water and mortal to divine –
There he is with piercing dart, union of the hearts.

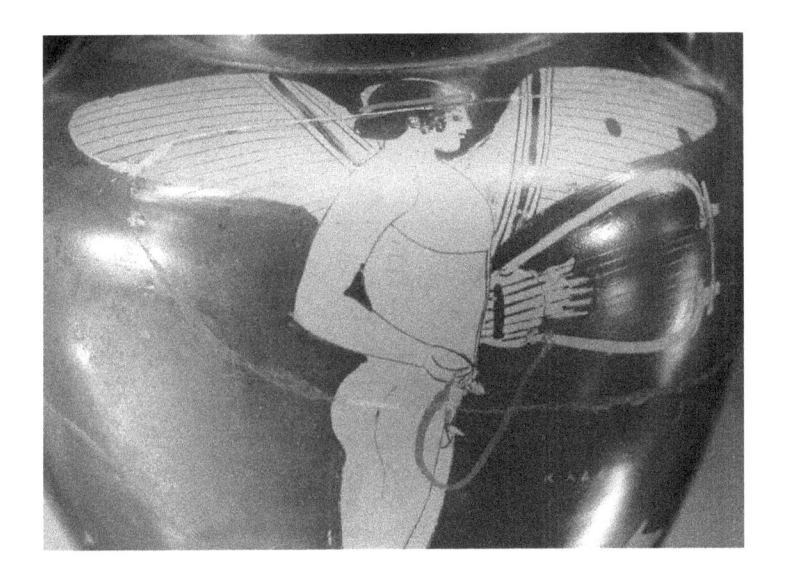

Eros and Psyche

Within the garden rests a soul, so beautiful by fair
She sped away the hour there beneath parental care
And how the watchful eye did observe wherever she would rest
To protect an exotic flower blooming within the mortal nest.
How she was loved by the honey-dripping bees
That a face full of grace and the sweet embrace of her arms
Was matched equally by the purity of her soul's charm
Not as a shady bramble, pulling away its twisted head from the light
Nor the golden narcissus gazing to the pond from its proud bed
There she grew, the tender bud nodding to the sun
The virgin-pale rose protected, nurtured, and beloved.

In the shadow of night Eros came to her bower
And fell victim to the consuming dart of his power
There, pricked, he spied the mortal butterfly
Slumbering as night's breeze fanned her wings of lace.
In that bed where innocence, the soft-sighing temptress
Welcomed in love the dark shrouded-divine embrace
Her eyes were blinded in the hours that he rested by her side
Sightless, her heart opened to the gift received by his kiss –

Drawing her within by his art to dwell forever within his heart
The mingled sighs upon one breath between two parted lips
There lay Psyche to Eros upon the fragile bloom
A nurtured golden flower slowly unfurling immortal petals by love
With each drop of heavenly rain open its tender tongue.

But light-winged butterflies, dancing their brief time
Will turn one morning on an errant wind and spin away
And so Psyche was torn from her love's embrace
To endure what was wrought by the light of day
No singing illusions of twilight and dusk could give her comfort,
No darkened cave could entice her to abandon what she had known
And none could entreat to her heart to pull it back to the mortal abode.
There she took flight, bearing aloft the brightness of her mortal light,
Following the traces of his hand upon the nations of the land
Her soul it pulled and yearned, and always drew her on
To seek him, the sweet kiss and immortal breath of her soul
And taste the nectar upon her lips and end suffering's travail.

To Aphrodite's labor she poured her heart, every task and hour,
Every weight that would crush her soul and break her wings,
He was there, his hand cupping hers, beneath his veil of invisibility
And lifted up her heart when it stuttered in lament beneath her task,
Ever at her side as she traveled upon her trial's sharp-stoned road.
Her tears stained her face even as unrequited love marked her heart
'Til she made her way to the door of the dead to greet Haides' bride
And sleep claimed the living light from the beauty of her eyes.
There Eros draws out his butterfly from her standing tomb
Awakened she draws in a breath, floating on the winds across the sea
To the heavens of Zeus Supreme, from the edge of dark cavern stream
The son of Aphrodite – bright-browed groom and his shining bride!

There the wife becomes again the bride, by the touch of immortal wine
The old bridal gown falls away, and all the ash of humanity fell

Aphrodite drapes golden veil to arise the beauty of the girl divine
There that all the gods did attend and drew up the bride of love
Pythos who revealed the weighted scales and Hermes the deliverer
Among the paired circle of harmony, there Eros and Psyche as one
For as a butterfly would emerge with flaxen wings to greet the sky
So gold-winged Psyche arose within Eros' timeless embrace
And there he flies resplendent with his heart and soul.

Helios

Helios is the titan of the sun. Whereas Apollon, a god whom he was later often confused with, is the light of the sun and ruler of the star, Helios is the spirit of the sun itself around which the earth revolves. The sun-chariot drawn by fiery mares is his, and was once drawn by his son disastrously. His ever-present eye during the daylight hours watches over all of the earth and was utilized by Hera in order to watch Leto so that she couldn't find some hidden place to give birth to her twins.

To Helios
The autumn birds sing their final song, a hymn of turning time,
Colorful wings against the sky following their shining lord.
And the birds that roost in the summer ponds like an arrow speed away,
Point a far-flying course to another land; a summer waiting to begin.
The yawning trees nod their heads in the blowing breeze,
Bow and farewell to the departing sun riding the horizon low,
Until the unshorn one arises when spring has come,
Leaving the horizon below.
Only the far-riding orb shall soon be seen,
Riding over a far-dwelling land,
At the world's edge in the distance rising;
Over the horizon brightly cresting.

The sun is carrying his bright torch, traveling across the sea,
The mountains, forests and grassy plains sing welcome and farewell.

See the laughing nymphs preparing their mossy winter beds,
They send kisses like sparrows on fair wings, to grace his golden cheek.
That to their company he would return,
Rising up again from the other lands,
To dance with them in the forests,
Upon the mountains and at sea's edge.

Return again to their charm,
To lie in happy state within perfumed arms,
And there they will spin their loving web
Upon boughs of flowered beds.
But there they sing their haunting song,
Farewell to the traveling sun,
Bright blooms to their cheeks from the frost of dawn,
In beauty they sing.

The sun is carrying his bright torch, traveling across the sea,
The mountains, forest and grassy plains sing welcome and farewell.

In the dark season of night,
The day is a brief melody dancing low in the sky,
And here the crystalline mirror, winter's gift,
Reflects his heavenly flame.
O dweller in the distant lands,
Bright sun caressing another loving face,
Dancing and singing to some foreign song,
Beloved to distant nations great.
O how you bright shine, at the horizon's edge,
Delighting in foreign company,
A great feast that you host and attend,
Where honey and wine like rivers run!
And there where the flower-crowned maidens
At your side happily attend,
A maiden, lover and bride,
Sings so sweetly her otherworldly song,
Bathing at the flowing spring,
Where she washes her perfumed hair.

The sun is carrying his bright torch, traveling across the sea,
The mountains, forest and grassy plains sing welcome and farewell.

Joyous song arise from the trees, from the mountain and valley heart,
The spring has dawned, and lo into the heavens steps the Sun,
Brightly crowned he rises with the golden rays upon his regal head.
Welcoming the tender lover's kiss of spring, a bud in youthful bloom,
A promise of fruitful summer within the sway of her hips,
Greeting her lover, the warm sun he stirs her blood,
Upon the bed of innocence.
The seeds of life race across the land,
Flower and fruit destined to bloom,
Upon the vine the fruit swells to ripeness, and to the sun flowers turn,
And the bride washes her hair in the spring, blossom-crowned.

To Helios II

Morning rises over the east,
Winged dawn stretches for her shining hand,
The morning star rests in the sky,
In faded night, a beacon to the rising sun.
See the bright streaks of fiery manes,
The mares lift into the heavenly dome,
Night withdraws with a gusty sigh
And farewell bids the pale descending moon.
For there amid the trumpets of morning
That greets the chariot's ascent,
Bright-crowned Helios,
From the golden Okeanos-held castle, rises in the holy east.

Hail bright-belted golden son, beloved of radiant-shining Hyperion,
Hail to your might, a light burning so bright, flame-crested rising sun.
Before you darkness flees away
And covers with dark lace her midnight face,
She sinks to bower releasing the heavens to her blue-gowned sister Day.
Turning time alights on your heavenly path,
Following steadily behind the wheel,
He measures the distance of passing hours

By where in the sky your mares fly.

The heavens shudder in delight
As over the horizon you crest traveling hence west,
Before your greatness the night-born stars fade
And hide their gleaming face.
The slumberous world flushes with color,
And the morning birds are quick to rise,
Arise, arise, they sing into the sky;
Awaken sleeping world for dawn has come!
The birds are singing with the risen song,
From Apollon's lyre steadily thrum.

Violet-robed, gold-shining god,
The heavens eagerly draw with welcoming arms,
The heated flames caress you of the chariot sun,
As you steer the delicate course,
The reins the mares pull eagerly taunt,
To plunge to the seas or burn down the skies.
The bitter regret for a proud son
Is well remembered by the heavens and seas,
To boil away or to fire and flame,
This was the price for the youthful capture of the reign.
To your charge, Elektor, this course is set,
And this daily route is ever in yours to keep.

Who can gaze upon you?
Your radiance pierces the eyes, senses and the heart,
Tearful eyes gaze up in adoration to you
As they clock your movement in the skies.
And high above time stands still,
The noon hour flares in brilliant light and heat,
A song rises from the earth, a bell tolls its noontime song,
And men go to their rest.

So bright the skies on your traveling path,
The flowers nod heads towards your form,
Faces up-turned, the blossoms follow
Your far-trekking heavenly western path.

But then the evening hour comes,
And in the west you arrayed in colors sink to rest,
The bright songs treble at the dusk,
A sweet farewell to your splendid, shining orb.
As a wearied traveler bows his bright brow,
And light fades to a slumberous dark,
Rush home on the winds, at the edge of the world,
To the welcoming west you descend.
The hooves on the mantled clouds crash
A blooming color of wine, of rose and pink flower.
Your gold-bright mares, foam-flecked,
Descend to west, and you sink to your nightly rest.
And there you sink down, and then around,
To come and to the east arise again!

Selene

Selene is the titan of the moon, and like Helios she was often confused with Artemis who was linked to the light of the moon, and later confused also with Hekate. Selene is the mother of the months and days as the ancient Hellenic calendar was a lunar-based one where the month was born on the new crescent moon and ended on the dark of the moon.

To Selene
Fair maidens, violet-crowned, ease upon your flowery beds
And sing a night's lullaby,
Sing now of the pearl-faced moon, crowned, horned,
With her dewy locks.
Mene is attended, beyond the horizon,
From perch of her resting satin bed,
There her bright-faced daughters,
Children born to Helios, kiss upon their mother's brow.
And from sweet company of Endymion's embrace,
Her lily-faced daughters, the months,
They rise to their mother's wide-armed embrace,
To the track the passage of time's walk.

She rises from the ocean, and the tides rush and spray,
Loath to part her from their grasp,
And so they follow her monthly course,
Reaching forth, yearning to touch that blossom face.
In the horizon she rises as a swan in flight,
Water dripping from her shimmering arms,
And her voice calls like a dove's lull;
Aloft into heaven's dusky arch, her milky mares wing.
As she travels on her course and caresses in her path
The father god in the heavenly sky,
From the swell of her body drops the sparkling daughter,

Ersa, begotten of the seed of Zeus.

Hail Mene, lamp of dusk, maiden eye of night,
Men look upon you with praise upon their lips,
Under the round orb of your shining crown,
A soft light filtering down, does the lover woo.
If even for a moment in time,
To lay a kiss upon the upturned tender sweet face within the light,
Just as you would steal a breath upon the secret slope,
To drop a kiss to fair Endymion.
You light the way to the lover's bed,
As your fullest brilliance marks true the hunter's path,
No prey is sweeter to be found
Than the kisses and sighs whispered from a beloved mouth.

Daughter of Hyperion, queen of the slumberous night
Adorned in ropes of luminous pearls,
Your pale light illuminates all and far outshines
All other nightly travelers beneath velvet skies.
Hail to you who bathe life below in a silver glow,
Like a touch upon a shimmering metallic sea,
And there the footsteps of Ersa, under that tender light,
Dances dew upon the flora standing.
The blooming blossoms hail to you, and cup the watery drops,
And from their lips it is sipped by the singing bees,
And those small-winged and wandering kin
Who drink from the laden petal.

Hail Selene, bull-eyed goddess,
As the time-spun month wanes, you pull forward your veil,
There you hide your shining face,
But even then your beauty surpasses the shining stars!
And you hide away, perhaps following Hekate's path
To darker worlds unknown to be lit,

Now hear the sigh upon the breath of wind,
A whisper plea for your rekindled torch.
Again you resume your monthly course,
And ignite again with embers of the sun,
For Helios strikes anew his blazing flames
As shining-eyed each month ascends, by your rise it marks.

Your light is a gentle glow, against the radiant beams of Helios,
Borrowed from his golden hall,
It is as the touch of a mother, in a gentle sweet embrace
Where a newborn babe is cradled.
But though you race, you do not flee far away
From your brother's gold-armed embrace,
Below he descends into the west, and you bid him sweet night,
And climb to your golden throne.
He does catch you, and the twin torches smolder,
Darkens and brightens the heavenly dome,
You, devoured and devourer, the seasons delight in their parents
Who then draw away and depart.

Depart and return, let loose your voluminous skirts
To circle round beyond the glowing crown,
Then in the height of your fair-cheeked beauty
Beloved by mortals and gods, withdraw and veil.
Your cycles manifest a calendar of the passage of time,
As your wide-browed face you turn about,
And like a shell from the heart of the sea,
Pale colors play off your fair countenance in their array.
Hail to you, star of the sea, hail to you, mother of hundreds,
Like Theia your embrace spans wide,
And therein, beneath the milky moonlit folds of light,
Your shimmering arms embrace many.

To Selene II

Hail to you, jasmine-crowned, bright-faced Selene,
The Muses and Nymphs aid this night-swept song,
To the heavenly throned nocturnal queen.
How sweet the smile that graces your face,
And the shimmer of liquid eyes beneath a pearly brow.

Holy Selene, you are like the blooming phlox flower,
Your fragrant pale skirts billow like the fragile petals,
And you are the sweet axis, dripping with heavenly honey.
You drip nectar, from the sky's embrace, the falling dew,
Your daughter, your nurturing essence, nursing the earth below.

Fair Selene, lover of many who seeks you among your pillowed bed,
Your abalone arms glowing in the night open wide to embrace.
There you are mother of hundreds who suckle at your curved breast!
Hail to the nurturing mother, your rounded form draws forth life,
And when the petals from the blossom have fallen seeds swell within.
The glow from you crown wreathes your head, pollen of the night,
And where moon-glow settles a night magic stirs and unfurls within.

For the moon is like a flower, a bud tightly wrapped unfolds,
And that bud of midnight grace, blooms her flower of a face.
But a flower wilts and the petals drop slowly, silently away,
And away the night hides your dark lace-veiled face.

Prometheus

Prometheus is probably one of the best known Titans; he is attributed with creating mankind and for his affection for humanity smuggled fire from Olympos to the earth. For this he earned a punishment from Zeus to be chained and have his liver devoured daily by a vulture until he was freed by Herakles.

To Prometheus
Mankind groaned at heavy loss when the chain was laid,
Binding down the immortal one to the unforgiving mountain top.
Weeping daughters perfumed the shrines, to soften the anger of Zeus,
To no avail, Prometheus was bound tight to the jagged rock.
Suffering immortality when death cannot deliver from the pain,
Continually to suffer, not a moment of relief or respite.

Great titan born of Tethys, the earthen womb, hail Prometheus,
And from the clays with gentle hands fashioned men of mothers' flesh.
Zeus' breath brought in life, Prometheus housed the flickering soul,
Infant men, weak and defenseless to nature's course,
So tenderly loved and cared for under a father's administrations.

A father willingly suffers, foreknowing the pain that is brought,
For happiness of the children made, all is worth the cost.
Gifts are given for good growth of the mortal-born little ones,
That we may know happiness in our shortened days,
And in our arts truly express the greatest gifts of civilization attained.
A father sees that his children never hunger in body or in soul,
That stomachs are healthily full, inspiration and thought filling minds.

What cost to him, to give the needed feasts to the earthborn men,
Sacrifice's bountiful meats, while the bones and fats the gods do keep.
What cost to a loving father to teach the children of happy civilization,
The flaming fired was in need, to bake the bread from Demeter's grain,

To forge the tools to turn the earth and protect and motherland.
That light would kindle minds and hearts and create safety's harbor,
Beasts shy away from the flickering flame – a welcome home it creates.
Warm fire, bind family about the hearth, welcome the dead to earth,
A treasured gift withheld, so a crafty father's minded calculated well.

Racing from heavens with burning light, a hidden torch burning bright,
That the gods may not too swiftly notice the flames had been stolen.
Necessity brought wings to his feet, light descending to men,
And at the first mortal hearth Hestia was kindled in the heart within.
Mortal hearts lifted high, and spread the flames among their kin,
Lighting familial hearths and tending to the arts at the heated kiln.
Good news and good things swiftly descended from heavens to men,
Rejoice and keep in hearts the worthy gifts
Of a father's love for mortal children.

No longer suffering, Prometheus guides,
Forethought given as good advice,
To well consider beforehand every action's fateful consequence,
And never in arrogance take for granted the arts
And fall into baseness of the worst.
Civilization and all things under her gain
All owe a great debt to Prometheus,
And so before him let humanity spirit lift to celebration
And leave forgotten woe,
The games lighten hearts of men
And those fires bind the kingdoms as one,
No anger, no bloodshed,
Arms put aside at the kindling fires of civilization's sport.

Leto

    Leto, often depicted modestly holding her veil, is said to have been from the Hyperborean region and is the mother of the twins Apollon and Artemis. Because of Zeus's affair with her, Hera would give her no peace and she was made to wander the lands looking for a birthing place. However, at every place she was turned away. Artemis was said to have been born at Ortygia and Apollon at Delos. Her children often defended their mother from rape and insult.

To Leto
Veiled Leto, most revered mother
Concealed in the dance of twilight,
Her light-born children attend to her
With a kiss and their arms embraced
Golden-browed Apollon upon his seat
Before the altar of the Dorian race
And quick-darting Artemis
Harnessing her steeds for their flight.
Far-shining twins beloved of a mother's heart
Born upon holy Delos' bed.

All musai and kharites honor the dark-browed mother in their song,
She who lifted the shadow of her robe and issued two rays of light
As the dawn and the dewy moon rise shining from the gown of night
There the twins leapt from the seat of her gentle lap in youth's delight
And so pleased the boundless heart of the daughter of Koios.

Leto, most supreme among mothers,
Sheltered her young beneath her belt
As the groans of her pregnancy played
Among the tempo of her feet.
There the deep-girdled one would sigh
And clasp her child within its seat

And hold her bright-armed babes close to heart
As necessity drove her forth,
Since no place would allow her
To lay down her head by stream or fallow.

Bearing them safely beneath her breast she continued
For no place would bear her,
Not Thessalia, nor the island Kerkyra
Would offer her the infant's cradle.
Twelve and again, days and nights
With sharp labor's gusty sigh until Delos offered respite,
Where Eileithyia unbound the cord
To draw forth the young, nine days born Apollon,
And his sister Artemis, to the mother's assistance,
Born those days minus one.

Never a mother who so greatly tended
To her sacred duty and so greatly loved,
Who bathed them with gentle hand in Lycia's waters,
Lifting them with kindly arms,
And her laughter rings out sweetly
And her great heart rises to see their play and charm
As Apollon lifts either bow or song
And Artemis on swift feet to the woods is borne,
To return and rest their heads upon her knee
Where she strokes their golden locks.
Great is Leto the mother, loving and ever-watchful
Within the halls of Apollon and Artemis.

To Leto II

O most revered mother, O goddess kindly gowned,
A banner of stars rests as your bright crown.
Sweetest daughter of bright-shining Phoebe,
Gentle light at dusk, gentle light at dawn,
Nurse-mother of the bright-flamed twins whom the world does love.
Fair-browed, fair-ankled, glorious Titan daughter,
Your holy womb nurtured twice the bounty of life,
And labored twice the hardship that birthing women endure.

Bless our wombs to be fruitful, to safely carry the seed to labor's end,
And to birthing cries may your bright-armed daughter swiftly descend.
Mother of best of daughters, may our daughters be of her like,
Bring pride to our hearts and self-surety strength to her dance.
O blessed mother of a strong-hearted beautiful daughter,
Grant us goodly daughters to bring company to our loving hearts.

Most loved mother, best of nurturers, protect our happy young,
As you protected daughter and son, usher Apollon to protect little ones.
A mother can do no more than see to a child's blooming good health,
There that they grow strong of body and healthy in all limb.
Nurture children, watch them grow, be the aid of mothers who pray!

Happy mother of a devoted son, twice blessed too with a daughter loyal,
Bless earthly mothers with good-hearted young, no greater prize is won
Than the child who brings pride to heart and family
By way of their minds and love.
Most blessed of mothers, hear our earthly maternal prayers.
Most holy of mothers, bring us the greatest gifts and ease future's years.
You who knew suffering for the infant's sake, shelter us from sorrow,
Bring mothers to comfort's bed; in safety generations are born and bred.
To you all happy mothers pray, most holy mother Leto!

Hekate

Hekate, a well-known torch-bearing goddess, is closely related to Artemis. Though there has in the past been some confusion between Artemis and Hekate, usually from Roman sources, Artemis is her cousin, Hekate's mother Asteria being a sister of Leto. Hekate is the leader of the hounds, goddess who leads the dead, and goddess of the month's end as the calendar transitions to the new month. When Persephone was kidnapped by Hades, Hekate was said to have heard her cry out as he carried her away and assisted Demeter in her hunt for her daughter. Come spring, Hekate with Hermes leads Persephone back. Fertility of the flocks and great catches of fish to fishermen were also attributed to her. At some point later she was depicted as a three-formed goddess.

To Hekate
Swathed in Red is Hekate.
Hooded in Red is Hekate.
Silver-hemmed Artemis, lift aloft your burning torch,
And bring the trumpet of the hunt.
The flow of life is in the hands of Hekate,
And her burning light guides the way.
Terror-ridden roar of the bull is the trumpet's blast,
And the hounds bay in search of their prey.
The beasts of the woods shudder in their homes,
And a cry fills the night air.
None is set apart from the hunt,
And Hekate guides the host of souls to their new abode.
The light of Hekate does not flicker,
But illuminates the halls of the dead,
And exalts in the company of fair Persephone.
Scarlet Hekate, we leave your monthly feast,
At the site of your throne.
Red-swathed Hekate has all roads lain before her,

And merciful goddess greets those unfortunate to share her plate.
The touch of Hekate is merciful, and in her embrace we depart.

To Hekate II

Hekate I sing of thee, night crowned Trimorphis at the gate,
Night-loving, night-dwelling, triple-crowned are you.
O thunderous-eyed goddess, red-hooded, red-veiled,
White is your gown in the underground, you a vein of light,
Goddess who pierces mercifully the darkest place of night.

Phosphoros, a heavenly queen, girt in your immortal shine,
The stars yield to your burning yew in their heavenly course,
Mapping out the seasons for the farmer's seed and knife,
Good guide of weather-worn sailors on their oceanic route.
And on your star-girded throne you draw the temptress night,
Hiding well the lover's embrace, handmaiden of Aphrodite.

To the light the oceans and river sing, moist-limbed Hekate,
They rush and draw about you as a lover would caress,
A stir of life resounds within its waves and watery breast.
The fish of the sea, and the aquatic beasts, do increase,
Within the net, or revoked, proud fisherman's blessed gain.
You walk upon the water, kissing upon with your silver light,
And there upon the beach you lay, to Khrysorrhapis' delight.

Companion of Oiopolos, to the fruitful beasts of men you attend,
Khthonie you arise among the flocks, young arrive to your embrace,
Sweet lullaby of life over the fields, earth's tender loving song.
And the caverns shake and open wide before your descending path,
Within your domain lays the riches and wealth treasured by man,
But to your ghostly-armed embrace, rushes the long dead race,
The spirited deceased to you come, O divine bright-coiffed Aidonaia.

To Hekate III

Sure-footed dog is the guide,
Of her friend; men that trail behind.
Dark-haired Hecuba wailed her grief,
And into Hekate's company she does keep.
The cry of the hound marks the path,
Mortal trails and the death's own road,
And there Hekate rises to the lead!

The cries of the hounds shake the earth,
The living scurry with fear alive in the breast,
For that eerie call does boldly announce,
That winding train of ghostly company.
At the head bright-crowned Hekate flies,
To lead the pack of shadows; departed dead.

A burning torch in the night is a single guiding light!
Brighten the shining light of the moving stars,
Spark of flame to the moon's own glow,
And then descend, descend to that world below!
How many guided? Countless on their course!
A ship is tossed blindly at sea, but the stars show the way,
Dotting a path on the heavenly map, a true compass to weary hearts!
Like sand through fingers time does swiftly pass,
Not lost in a churning wind, the moon shows the day.
The twisted flaming yew grips fair slim hand,
Tracking guide through the heavens, seas and land!

But when the day comes and ends, there she still leads,
Ever at the night-wandering company of the blessed deceased.
Below, below on Hades long-traveled road,
Then to rise, guiding springtime Persephone with her light!

To Hekate IV

Silence upon the lips, blinded are the eyes
To come at night to the place where Enodia resides
Hear the holy music resound, the drum beats,
The sigh of air they sing. Hear the music of your soul
Vibrating from deep within by instruments nature gave.
Your silent song rising to the night
At the place where offerings are lain.
That where dark conceals, her light reveals
And shine the torch upon the paths and roads
Illuminating but a small space of endless void
The place of hidden beyond mind and eyes.
There the ghost dog watches by your side
Eyes soul-lit under the dark moonless skies,
A thing of loyalty to mankind, faithful guide,
Little hound of Skylakagetis leader of the twilight dogs
As little stars that would run across the midnight heavens
Sparkling flares of light to guide weary travelers home.
All those souls lift their eerie whisper on the breeze
As they leap through concealed streets where the ways meet
And the bygone old has been laid to its death
Dressing in bright purity traveling upon the higher roads
Hekate welcomes the road-walkers to her plate at her feast.

IV
Other Gods

This final section is devoted to the "lesser" gods of Hellenismos, the gods of the fields and streams, intricately tied to our environments, muses, nymphs, and deified children and lovers of the gods. These gods may not get a lot of large-scale public attention, but they are often important parts of domestic and localized worship. There are of course gods such as Pan who, while not being one of the major gods in the Hellenic pantheon, has gained a lot of attention and popularity among worshippers. In that light, though this section is relatively small, I feel it is important to begin it with Pan.

Pan

Pan is the goat-horned god, identified occasionally with both Dionysos and Apollon. He, like these gods, is an oracular god who was said to have sacred caves devoted to this function. He is connected to the woodlands, god of shepherds, an adorer of nymphs, and is often depicted carrying his reed pipes. He was considered something of an unattractive god who was able to inspire laughter in the other gods around him.

To Pan

Haunting meadows, Ekho whispering across the valley fertile,
Wild-eyed nymphs flee in laughing sport from Pan double-horned.
Beloved of all the deathless gods, wild-crowned son of Epimelios,
The prankish-loving, shepherd-adoring, nymphs play just beyond,
The wily, goat-hoofed god whom vigilant shepherds adore!

Sing with charmed delight, Muses all. To this son come and gather,
To the far-sprung meadows, among the lonely speckled hills,
Butterflies flutter and in gust air play, little dancers spinning.
Dionysos perhaps does not rest too far, whose company Pan adores,

For he can be often found at the side
Of the vine-wreathed laughing lord.

Hail Pan, hail Nomios, at the forest edge,
Grassy hills and mountain embrace,
Great haunter of your rich terrestrial domain, your pipes hidden sing.
As you drive the wooly bleating herds, Phorbas, panic you drive.
Wildly, crashing through, panic takes wing before your risen staff.
Perhaps it is credit due to your pipes and their ghostly singing tune,
What laughing delight you take in the rushed endorphins of fright,
That causes men to strip away the civilized, and dart about like beasts.

Wild-maned, craggy-browed, a curving smile, a mocking grin,
Kindly bountiful god, Agrotas, laden with the earth's great wealth,
O how the Earth smiles at your antics, and with laughter shakes,
For the prancing lifting gate as you dance in Bacchic celebration!
But to her gift you do acclaim, and at your cave wisely speak.

Dance of Pan

Little horns ivy-crowned,
Sweet perfume of the flower's nectar
Running down his prancing limbs.
Happy he dances to the leaping song,
In Bacchic company on the mountain side.

And there the nymphs crowned summer blossoms,
Wearing wreaths upon slender arms and lovely brows,
They wrap the scented garland in sweet drapes,
Upon the ground where the gods do dance.

The birds trill in the air to the pipes' dainty song,
Measured to a beat of the clip of little hooves,
And the rhythm of the Cybelline drum,
To the wild maenadic songs from softest lips.

Little shower of fragrant blossoms,
Blowing on the laughing breeze,
Tangled in his wild hair dancing upon the wind.

Beasts of the forest take up and dance,
Leaping along to his wood-wind song.
The speckled fawn, and the lion cub,
Dancing, dancing to a wild song of life and death.

And his song turns to mournful sleepy tune,
And all lay down to rest under blanket of twilight,
Drifting along with their eyes raised to the skies,
There the song does not end but the stars gracing heaven,
Make appearance one by one and don their brightest gowns.

There they spin around, in a slow swaying dance,
Twinkling bright, the diamonds on their crowns,
Dancing to the symphony of the night, of Pan's song.

Hades

Hades is the Lord of the Underworld and keeper of the dead souls. He is the youngest brother of Zeus and Poseidon; when they drew lots to split the world, Hades was the unluckiest and got the Underworld. He is a god of great underground wealth, and his realm is guarded by the three-headed hound Cerberus. Hades fell in love with Demeter's daughter Persephone and abducted her, but she later became his Queen and they rule together peacefully.

Hymn to Hades

Khaire Hades, regal master upon your rooted throne
Twisting silver and golden limbs from the hallow earth
Amid an ebony-dark palace encompassed by Styx's girth;
And upon your midnight locks is a luminescent crown
Set with the gems of fire and ice born in the world below.
At your court all life rests and takes its final earthy bow
As you, most kindly father, welcome and embrace all.

The fruit has fallen to the ground, and the withered vine
Brushes twining fingertips upon russet leaves and snow
And in the air all around there is a peace, of a kind
Where the swan-downed bard makes his winter rounds
Beside the golden glow of the hearth's fireside.
Your stern lips curve in sweet mirth at the singer's lull.

There grinning Death smiles to you, O kindly Hades
The ice rattling from his sleeves mellows to dew
As he passes by your mighty halls with his retinue,
All mortal life birthing, living and passing to its ends,
Your million children that Night's son merrily sends
To your endless kingdom, bearer of all wealth,
The house of the winter seed and the hunter's call.

Hypnos

Hypnos is the god of sleep, the son of Night, and brother of Thanatos (death). In the world of dreams there are supposedly two gates, one ivory and one made of horn; one gate contains prophetic dreams and the other false dreams.

To Hypnos
Muses, sing your slumberous song to the friend of men.
Dark-browed Hypnos, son of deep-bosomed Nyx,
Visit on the wings of night, to embrace the race of man.
Your kindly arms draw us down, but in that abode not to stay,
For Thanatos, your night-born twin, reaps us to arise never again.
But to your touch we gratefully lean to soothe the wearied mind.

Happy companion to Leader of Souls, opener of the gateways,
And there to your touch another opens,
To allow the oneirii passage through.
Morpheus attends to the dreams, in which we actors play our part,
But his power waxes and wanes under province of your own great art.
You chain the power of your children, attend to their devious games.
Sway them against the ivory gate, and let the horn open wide!

Hypnos, in your shadowed arms we happy people rest,
For in your absence our minds would be consumed, and made home
A dwelling for madness to make her triumphant bed.
Hail to you Hypnos, who draws us away into the slumber-land.

Iris

Iris is a messenger of the gods, particularly connected to Hera. She is the rainbow arcing from the heavens to the earth as she descends.

To Iris

All children born of mortal womb love and adore
The goddess who dances upon heaven's dew
And the fair-tressed Muses take delight to sing
Of Iris, alighting on the roads between light and rain
The dewy drops lingering still after a season shower,
There she spreads wide her colored veils
As golden wings whisper drawing the colored ribbons nigh,
Dancing on the heavenly light of the sky.
There beneath the breath of summer's day
She bathes her limbs in the water's spray
Rising from the seas, or drifting along the breeze
Of the waterfall sheltered among trees
Where her unbelted gown and loosened veils
Shimmers arching gracefully down
Like beautiful wisps of tattered ribbons loved by the sun,
There for a moment – and then gone.
For three seasons she dances across world,
But winter's ice too holds her gold
That as the sun kisses the water diamonds of ice and snow
There she plays for all to behold
Swiftly darting upon the crystal facets,
Uncatchable rainbow of light's tempered fragments.
To iridescent-eyed Iris we sing adoration,
Quick-footed beauty beloved of all of earth's nations
Begotten of amber Elektra and sea-eyed Thaumas,
She who raises the heavenly vase
To draw up the leaping water from her father's abode
To her mother's pillowed home

The sweet droplets heaven-shaking Zeus sends down,
Heaven's gift upon the ground,
Iris bearing the heavenly cups of the Olympians,
Fair messenger of the gods, and from gods to men.

Muses

There are nine muses, all beloved of Apollon, who preside over the arts, science and humanities.

To the Muses
There they dance, the muses nine,
Bright daughters of Zeus and Mnemosyne
Scarce had they been born
That they jumped up and began to sing;
Those tender maidens of gentle mean.
Whispering words upon four winds,
Remembering, inspiring wells of knowledge,
And Musagetes, nine days born
And nine of power, leads their choir
Breathing the song of the universe,
Bearing up the children singing holy verse
For each kiss they part on the mortal brow,
There their gifts they bestow
As a raindrop falls upon the ground
And sows rich the earth,
A song without sound, a melody of creation,
Of a birth, there the Muses sow holy words
Among the living breath, a sweet sigh
In time, of humanity's nation.
Star-eyed ladies, eons turn and to the ages
They sing at the grotto of Helion
And everywhere too they reach their hands
To mortal hearts spanning moral lands.
Never a child of science or art
Been born who closed their eyes
And refuted to have spared
A shy glance toward their divine form
Nor lacked the hidden mark,

The brand of their caress,
Rousing awake a holy spark,
Drawing us forward to sing
In great favor of the muses nine:
Inspiration of the sacred past,
Melpomene bearing the weeping mask;
And there dark-eyed Cleio
Drawing up the scrolls of the history;
Polyhymnia beloved of
The company of the bardic priests;
Terpsichore bringing choral dance and song
To the occasion of the holy feasts;
But to Urania astronomers,
With concerted gazes
To the heavens, pay heed
And great writers bow to Calliope
For the tales of heroic deeds;
Euterpe is in poetic dance of the lyric song,
With Erato there they laugh,
And too Thaleia jests with them
Bearing her merry mask and staff.
Hail to you, beloved Muses nine,
Weaving upon the song of Apollon,
Hail to you inspiration divine.

To Clio

I sing now to you solemn Clio,
Bearer of the scrolls,
The winding path of history
You have recorded and tracked.
History is a kind thing,
Oft neglected and ignored,
Men doomed to repeat,
If to your soft word they do not heed.

You are the watcher of passing days,
Like a still and rooted tree,
And your voice is a soft rustle of the breeze
Playing among the leaves.
The hide scrolls, or the parchment book it matters not,
For silently you watch and wait,
And record man's good and ill deed.

What many things there are for you to account,
Through the hands of men,
And though I may never be as fair
As you of word and speech,
Clio, if you grant me fine memory
Of that which has passed and gone,
When singing of far greater deeds,
I will honor you in my song.

To Polyhymnia

O sweet-voiced Muse, if but you would grace me with your song,
I would ever honor you in my hymns that that I set before the gods.
You set graceful fingers upon the lyre, pluck the sacred golden string,
And your voice raised like the holy wind, in a voice of myriad sound.
Your song is to and of the gods, it sings of all things that are holy,
This song filters down to voices of men, a sacred gift they might give.

When I listen to write my sacred verse, you lean in and whisper close,
And there your voice is like many celestial choirs layering upon another.
When I go to write, these words that you do inspire to sing,
Your hand touches mine and guides the fingers to write a fair harmony.
The harmony of the worlds spinning together, that ties all life as one,
And that the gods act together, weaving a far greater masterpiece.

Hail to you, many-voiced Polyhymnia, deliverer of most sacred gift,
Within your blessings we learn to lift our voices clear and loud,

To sing a song of gods, entwined and apart from the world of men.
The singers are blessed by your presence and loved of the gods,
Bring to girls sweet voices singing to willowy Artemis,
And to boys Delphinian songs, to unshorn Apollon sung.

Nymphs

Nymphs are female spirits associated with trees, rivers, springs, oceans and mountains. They are often the source of admiration for gods, satyrs, and shepherds. One well-known nymph from myth is Daphne whom Apollon fell in love with, but she was turned into the laurel tree in order to escape him by her father. Nymphs could also be deified lovers of the gods, such as in the case of Kyrene who was loved by Apollon when she went to fight the lion that was threatening her homeland. She became a lake nymph.

Daphne

The laurel crown, sweet spiced perfume,
Wafting from the tender glossy green,
The leafy band graces the victor's brow,
Great honors of the games, Pythian.
And sweet Daphne, her fragrant locks,
Plucked by loving golden hands,
Much beloved, in high honor, of Phoibus,
Woven together as the holy prize.

Fair, slender-limbed, river's daughter,
Graceful as the saplings curving bough,
A sweet fruit of her father, ripened in a flush,
The bright bloom of maidens for womanhood.
A great temptation for men who may spy,
In her father's meadow a bright flower blooms,
So much more for the god who is pricked,
By Eros' vengeful loving golden dart.

That which the golden lord did mock,
Of the delicate bow that delivers a mother's will,
He did learn in most painful exacting way,
The poison overpowering of the quit-cutting arrow.

Powerless against the love, an overbrimming cup,
To pursue the apple-cheeked, perfumed Daphne.
Passion gave him to wings to chase her far,
Across the earthly stones, a win so far and so near.

His heart lamented for the girl who would not stay,
Who flew like the august doe before the bow,
His appeals unheard, deaf to his soon-lover's ears.
A glimmer tear in his eye, for the love that would not wait,
For nor did he spy that lead arrow delivered true.
It found its marks, lodged within her downy breast,
To urge her on winged feet, away from pursuer – away.
What a sad fate to be, caught in a mad chase,
The prey ever fleeing, the hunter ever pursuing.

Bright eyes alight, the chase's end is nearing,
Golden arms outreach to catch and embrace,
The cherished lover who is slowly succumbing.
His catch in sight, a touch of warm flesh to his touch,
Heated hands curve round that delicate arm,
She is reaching, reaching, to her father sweetly imploring.
She cries out, the hunter is reaching, almost in grasp,
Dying, dying to that fearful touch – to be the last!

A loving father groans with his daughter's sweet cry,
Like a song of a mourning dove that falls to the hawk,
The river reaches up from his foamy rushing bed,
For a last time caresses his daughter's pliant flesh.
The flesh quivers and hardens, the color deepens,
A father weeps as his daughter graceful flying feet,
Bury for all time deep within the dark soil of nursing earth.
Rooted to place, embraced within the golden arms,
Barred against him by that crust of bark upon her flanks,
Daphne bows her leafy head against the gentle breeze.

A burning love snatched away, Apollo caressing the green,
The leaves to his touch release sweet perfume to the wind,
And warm the sorrowing heart of the far-shooting god.
The maiden lost, her beauty and essence forever remains,
Caught upon the wind whispering through the branches sweet.
A crush of leaves brought to his lips, breathing soft against his skin,
Daphne upon his breath, sweet herb of the Pythias.
With love he removes a garlanded fragrant branch up high,
And the leafy brow nods assent to the lover she did reject.
Though apart from him, a part of him to always be,
Most honored, most treasured, Daphne of the laurel tree.

To Kyrene

Maiden girl, strong of heart, upon the mountainside,
Had Artemis taught the huntress' art in your tender youth?
To brave the untamable wilds where men dare not,
To wrestle the bright-maned lion to the rocky sloping stone,
Strong of arm, strong of spirit, to protect the tender flock,
To draw the fated blood from the lion's tawny neck,
With not a weapon in your shapely hand!

Strong-limbed, bright-browed, were you a nymph in her company?
Delighting in the spear and flashing arrow to bring the beast to ground,
And how many hearts of gods did turn to see racing girls,
With wild cries and dancing steps across the mountainside.
Artemis prepared the way, rearing you in her wild arts,
Producing a spirit that would stay, to not be hindered by dreaded fear,
To not take to the wind and flee away, but to know the game of hunt,
And the fortune to which it ends,
This dance between hunter and hunted.

Why would not a god, when seeing your valiant spirit bright,
Not have the heart within his breast beat for you his bride.
He caught you from the mountainside, to tangle with a greater hunt,
Danger never sweeter than that loving hunter who draws in quick,
To capture his maiden huntress bride upon that high windy cliff.

To Apollo Creusa bore Ion,
And sprung a fair granddaughter, Chlidanope,
And she in grace bore you lovely nymph,
Born to capture a golden heart.
Apollo loved you upon windy Pelion,
And he loved you in the flowered bed,
Arranged so artfully by the pillow
And by the bloom of Aphrodite's blessed hand.
And there the bright-haired women in joy
Did dance to your marriage crown.

Hail to you most blessed among women, fire-sparking heart,
To you born a great generation, nurtured at the breast of the Earth.
Fortunate woman in Apollo's loving embrace, mortal-born nymph,
Apollo's tender gifts ran plenty for his love, his bright-eyed bride,
To your honor and affection
The nymphai dwell in company at your side.

To Kyrene II

Most noble Kyrene, golden-browed, lion-gowned,
Ferocious strength bound with feline claws
At the mountain top she stands so proud
A sash of blood worn, dripping to the ground.

Sprayed like flowers across her skin,
Her conquest marks her like a tattooed brand
As if Artemis painted her with a blazing brush
Ruby stains of the sunset upon breast and hand.

And she, so ragged, adorned in gore
That Apollo, bright lord, found her there,
Courageous light proudly glinting in her eyes,
In strength of her heart he found her fair.

In her battle he found her most glorious
In her triumph, her task done, union their hearts sought
Eros urging to place his kiss upon her shining lips
To finish in love what had long been wrought.

To the Dryads

A touch and kiss of the wind and the trees do sway,
Like dancers shifting their skirts in the touch of the breeze,
Nature's sweet harmony and eternal moving dance.
The Muses sing to these daughters of sturdy earth,
The nymphai of the wild-growing and domestic tree.
And the winds are captured in their long-armed embrace,
Mothers of air upon which beasts depend,
Against the ravages of harsh winds they too defend.

Many dryads as there are many trees that dot the earth,
Sisters united, but so different in fairness and in girth,
Endless living daughters, and those who rise and die.

Sad song for the races of hamadryad who is bound to her home,
That the tree that is swallowed or cut, so down she falls.
Dependent on the will of men, to whom she feeds her fruits,
The fruit-bearing trees may be culled, or dropped to ground,
And in death's cold grasp, she gives a last gasp as life ebbs away.
Hail to the fair-faced fruit and nut, of mulberry and stately oak.

But the evergreen, proud-bearing, wild mountain-growing,
The coniferous tree raises ancient branches along the mountain side.
Oreiades, ancient ones, who sprung from dance and wild mountainside,
Sheltering harbor of wild beasts, immortal protectresses of their own.
Dancing hand in hand, with their fair sisters the mountain's ash,
Earth-sprung daughters of Ouranos' blood and first mothers of men.
In company the Oreiades delight in the bearers of their fathers' shafts,
The speared-arms that protect the sacred place in mountains shade.

Hail to the dryads, earthly daughters
Many-formed and many-named,
Protectresses, mischief-makers,
In those mountains and groves they haunt.
Blessings spring to the orchard tender,
Grove keeper, and lonely shepherd,
Who tend well to their responsibilities
Upon the land the dryads keep.
Though they do delight in giving the lonely traveler a good fright,
Their laughter tinkles down in harmless delight from the shaking trees.
But when the wind changes from a caress to a raging mighty roar,
Seldom do the trees in their keep ever break – it is their nature to bend,
And protect the land under their guardianship that they endlessly tend!

The Nereides

Born of the ancient sea depths, pride of old father Nereus,
The fruitful fifty were born, bountiful children of the sea.
Daughters as fair as the foam, and the dawn after storm,
Dancing in the ocean-spray mists, kindly daughters of Doris.
At the edges of the sea, Muses sing of thee, most lovely sisters fifty!

I sing to you swift goddesses, nymphai playing among the waves,
Nymphai sitting and singing upon the jutting rising rocks.
A beacon you are to watchful men, signaling welcome shore,
Dear aquatic friends warning of the approaching tearing storm.
How fair you rise from the heart of the sea's watery embrace,
From the cave you rise astride,
Upon the fairest creatures of sea's own kind.

The fortunate may catch a glimpse of fair limbs as the wave does crest,
And few may see in the distance, a nereid on a rock sunning her breast.
The sweet child staring down into her face like a watery mirror,
Below may see beyond the reflection another face watching her.

Of the sea, and by the sea,
Woven into that deep watery abode,
In company of Tritones, at Poseidon's side,
Fabric of the blessed sea.
Foam-armed daughters,
You are the water's turning brimming life,
Propigate the beasts of the marine,
Greatest wealth of the bountiful depths.
The fish are many and steadily increase
And fill the nets with greatest ease.

Hippokampos crests the rolling waves, and in company dolphin plays,
Such gaiety of the calm sea, swiftly away as the storms roll turbulent.
The warning song alights over the roaring winds and thunderous crests,

Ships turned over and pounded by the raging storm, break and sink,
Descending down into the Nereids' watery home,
The grave the waters keep.
Fragile lives tossed in a raging sea,
May you lift the traveler from death's embrace,
Merciful daughters, for those the sea has slain,
Make comfort their rest,
Or return them from the depths
To the mother's weeping breast.

So much more than fair maidens
Directing the course of the changing seas,
From the ancient speaking lips,
You were weaned on many things.
The seas keep knowledge to men
Unknown, and you reveal,
That your train upon the sea,
First pilgrims of fair Persephone.
Whispered at the foamy shore,
Mysteries of Iakhos and rites of Kore!
And there upon the island reef,
Dance and play along the pilgrim way.

Hyacinthos

Hyacinthos was a prince of Sparta loved by Apollon for his unparallelled beauty and youth. He was immortalized when the discus Apollon threw him in error hit him in the head when the wind blew it off course. The hyacinth flower was born from the drops of his blood. In Sparta there was a festival for this god called Hyacinthia.

To Hyacinthos

Mortal life is a fragile thing, a winged butterfly scattered on a breeze,
Spun around in Fate's woven web, a verse and line in the Muses' song.
Sweetest kindled love, young blossom unfurling upon the earth,
Touches and warms the immortal heart, a flicker in a timeless span.
Flickering light so well beloved, bright sky-shining eyes of innocence,
Behold the boy at the gate, never to reach the manhood state.

Fair-locked Hyacinth, a fragrant sweet breath with every laugh,
Perfumed so perfectly in a puff from his bowed lips, nature-painted.
A delicate firm fruit ripens sweetly with its juice upon the limb,
But just short of that fulfillment of ripened flesh, to the ground it fell.
The wind must have blown it far too soon from that harbor safe,
And down it fell to provide a pearly feast for the creatures of the earth.
Sweetest Hyacinth, torn in love, from Apollon's laurel bough,
By the breath of pining jealousy – Zephyros, wind-flying god.

A small stir upon the wind can turn the course of flight to death,
And drop the small bright-winged soul to the dusty grit of earth.
No lover's cry and lament can draw it back to the skies,
Fading light, to the earth, the ground, never again to rise and fly.
A laughing game, turns to death, as the discus veers off course,
From Apollo's golden hand, the discus is delivered as a dart.
Unintentional death, unconceived of and much bemoaned,
That the blood flows from the heart as it stutters to a still.

Innocent blood upon the ground,
Staining a grisly rose upon the ground,
Sweet wretchedness is the perfume of life slowly away draining down,
And a god heart turned to sorrow rises from that blossom wound,
A flower to remember, in its brief bloom, innocent love sweet perfume.
Spring flower arises from the wrap of leaves,
A cone of flowers in the breeze.
So sweet and delicate every bloom,
Dyed from the birth of flowing blood,
Fleeting sweetness, and the blossoms wither, drop and fall away.
Tender spring flower, Apollon gathered to him and great grieved,
Pale, life-drained, a flower fading fast,
Cut from root under summer light.
And the risen flowers grieved with the god, in a lament's song,
Ever to lament in its brief beauty, marking a death of one so young.

Ariadne

Ariadne is the deified wife of Dionysos. She had assisted Theseus in leaving Crete only to be abandoned on Naxos where Dionysos found her. She had several children with her husband and is often portrayed reclining next to him.

To Ariadne
Grief-struck girl, abandoned, alone
Set aside so far from her dearest home.
Her flowered heart that brimmed with love,
Dashed away, rejected beneath the watching sun.
Her cry rises up like the most keening song,
That no lamenting bird could in truth rise to match.
A broken heart, adrift upon an ocean of deceit and lies,
Hope drifts away on that rolling steady current,
That so swiftly carried away love upon the morning tide.

The moon bore witness to the departure in stealth,
And Selene in her throne wept for the girl alone,
Abandoned in sleep upon that beach – that rocky ground.
The stars above Naxos hid their shining faces in sympathy,
And the sun above listens to pliant cries that rise in symphony.
A song of lamentation woven with the winds and rushing tides,
Set adrift alone upon that sea of deceit and lies.

Abandoned and cruelly turned upon, how fate does repeat,
That she who surrendered to love, the fate of her family.
The ocean's waves, the tides carry in and out the changes of time,
The grievous past borne out, and a new love carried upon the rise.
Spent in grief she lay upon that beach, seeing not the face of love,
Death is slow to those whose grieve and eats away at the dying dove.

Dionysos spies the waning bright, of her beauty's fading light,
His heart captured, weeps for her, his arms so willing steals her,
A love that will not be denied, to kidnap her away from Naxos' shore.
To a new home, in love's embrace she was happily borne,
Wooed with the sweetest wine-kissed lips of love-drunken Dionysos.
A marriage-bed gifted none to be sweeter; pale is the bed of Theseus,
For with Dionysos Ariadne rises,
Bound to him forever as his loving bride.

Happiness rises, sadness long forgot, hope and love refound,
And the bright-bloom flushes in delight with the love of His touch,
Immortal-gifted, treasured love, to her love reunited and reborn.
Aloft in the heavenly skies, when night wears her midnight gown,
The stars loop ring to form of Ariadne, the bright marital crown.

Adonis

Adonis was the lover of Aphrodite, and a boy of such beauty he was loved by both Persephone and Aphrodite. Because both goddesses loved him it was decided that he would spend a third of the year with Aphrodite, and a third with Persephone, and a third as he liked. As it happened he loved Aphrodite and chose to spend his third of the year with her as well. In some versions of the myth Apollon in an act of vengeance killed Adonis, but in another it was Ares motivated by jealousy that took the form of a boar and killed him. Adonis is the beautiful fragile life that comes before the killing heat of summer, and his death is mourned annually by followers of Aphrodite.

To Adonis

Adonis, boy, a tender spring shoot,
Seeded in a secret light of forbidden love,
Unblemished, stainless, in perfection born,
From Smyrna's deep root, the laboring womb.
Perfumed boy, waxing among the sweetest sap,
Delivered into the world, a blooming mortal flower,
Fated to live and love between earth and sea.

Garland-crowned prince, beloved of two queens,
A pale flower blossoms and then retreats,
Delivered between the golden arms as seasons turn,
A portion of year to Persephone, and beheld to Aphrodite,
And fair Love receives too his own third in bowered bed,

What insult to fan in the heart of crowned queen of the dead!
Tender boy playing hunter's fine made man,
Under careful watchful guidance of Aphrodite's leading hand,
Away, away the dangerous beasts that hunt night and day,
That this bright flower boy in her company always stay.
Love is a sweet thing, it disregards and lays aside,

Un-heedful of the needful things, for a time of sweetest bliss.
And that passion which flames up high beneath the kiss,
Strikes vengeful to those who against love transgress.

But summer heat devours the tender gardened plant,
And the fragile frond wilts beneath the heated blast.
That gold-flanked boar bit deep with his curving tusk,
The death-moan like a sigh of youth upon the wind,
And Adonis falls to death in his moist leafy bed.
Spiral up from the tear-wet blood, the blossom flowers,
Fragrant spring blossom, brief in life, Adonis lives anemone.

Weep and cry women, for the sorrow of Aphrodite,
Budding young love ripped from the light of life.
Sorrow with her wandering sorrow, at the side of the sea,
There with golden company, fling in mourning from rock into deep.
Garlands drift upon the waters, a fragrant blossom out of sight,
To the edge of the world, and in spring to come again.

Adonis, fair Adonis, half of the year beneath earth's breast,
Within Persephone's rich treasure-jeweled halls to grace.
And then rise again, rise again to Aphrodite's remembered embrace,
Sweet myrrh embalms and runs fast through trees in spring renewed.
Tender spring flower, brief life so sweet in the world of men,
And beneath raging sun, withered, descend and descend.
Adonis with Aphrodite here, and then so soon gone again,
Cry for grief of Adonis, you who ever loved, bright-cheeked women!

To Adonis II

The bane of summer with its leaching rays
Draws ever closer in the waxing days
Where once I rested my head upon the pillow of her breast
O the sweet cream beneath my parched lips
And she cupped the nectar of spring flowers within her hands

    And tipped that wine
      Down
              Upon my tongue
Now lamenting arms cannot keep me
As Helios lingers high above the world
The tender green withering beneath his gaze
So too do my fruitless arms
Unsteady in their youth
Turn back with a sigh to the earth
To sleep
To die
I am a blossomless sprout
Fair for its brief breath
And the fragile charm of sweetest days
I return ever to the bosom of our mother
Whom all humanity holds dear
Passing away to return
When the sun yields mellow warmth
Dappled between soft fronds of green
I return to the dewy violets
Of Aphrodite's succulent bed.

Semele

Semele is the mother of Dionysos conceived in union with Zeus. She was killed when Hera tricked her into asking Zeus to reveal himself in his true form to her. Later Dionysos traveled to the underworld to remove her from that abode.

To Semele
The tomb is crowned with ivy, a shrouded memento of time past
Where sweet strains of the Muse's songs could cloak it so delicately,
There was lain the mortal remains,
There was lain the gown and her hair unbound,
Her cheek no longer a shining pearl,
But scorched by heat of Zeus' arms
That she who would lay in lovers' union,
Walking down her road of fate,
Desiring his full glory to her bed to join with him
In bridal bed and beloved.
There Semele was consumed, fire burning:
Transforming the flower in its bed
When it turns to the summer sun,
It withers beneath the fiery kiss
And so, torches flaming upon her skin
Semele surrenders her withering flesh
To the power of Zeus' touch, agonizing ecstasy –
A burning current that strikes,
Overwhelming union of mortal and divine,
Closing her eyes her life flies away,
Till all that remained was the butterfly's hollow nest
And the child Dionysos.
Her grave is but a marker,
A memory for those who walk the living road
For she does not reside there
Where the dead dwell beneath the stone.

Hades ceded her long ago
From ever returning to those deep abodes,
Never to have that lifeless night
Obscure her sight and remove the sun
Nor again to walk along the mortal road
Along the twisting path to death:
Beloved Semele liberated and arisen –
Immortal in the fruit of her union!

To Semele II

Honored Semele, beloved of Zeus
Delicate butterfly drawn to the light
You walked in the palm of Hera's hands
Into the radiant glory of truth
As for a moment you rested in her marriage bed
And with your pearly arms and a prayer of happiness
Upon your innocent lips, drew in
Those burning flames presented in love.

Here is a seed of the mystery
Her rosy veil fades; threads of a setting sun
As the flames split the mortal shell
And his embrace renders her to shades of dust.
What he loves he touches
What he touches he transforms
Whither gone Io and Callisto,
From Semele's heart he bears forth
The Master of Changes
The infant with a promise budded upon his brow
Within his wintry cradle, his mother's grave.

Orpheus

Orpheus was the son of Apollon and famed poet, author of the Orphic hymn, and instructor in the mysteries. His music supposedly had a magic effect on all around him, which he used to retrieve his wife Eurydice when she died by charming Persephone with his song. Unfortunately, when he failed to follow instructions, he was unable to bring his wife to the world of the living, and lived in misery until he was torn apart by maenads. His head was said to continue to spout oracles after being severed from his body.

Orpheus, Gift of the Gods
He is like a bird, with a voice so sweet,
There sits beneath the drooping bough of the willow tree,
Singing with sparrow's song, rich-voiced song of Apollo.
Bright plumage, graceful form of such delicate feather,
Painted the colors of flowers beneath the light of dawn,
With the bloom of a summer rose upon his cheek,
And the violets shining velvety within his eyes, graced by Aphrodite.

Where he walks across the land the people come to gather,
That they would fain to hear the mystery that falls from his lips,
To the living spheres of sweet harmony that sing out to him in melody.
The flowers and the beasts bow their heads to listen to the song,
And the hearts of the folk are drawn like butterflies to threads of light.
Hear and Listen people carefully, words are hidden within words,
A lyric is not all of that which that is seems, there is an unknown song.

His moonlit feet have walked upon the many roads to return again,
And to our ears rises his blessed song, a gift from divine above.
Let butterflies rise to the skies to adorn themselves with golden wings,
That they may rest upon his shining brow to hear the immortal songs.
His heart travels where no other travels, seen beyond what is seen,
And here his message carries in a woven web with its hidden meaning,
That we may too strive to step beyond the fabric of these lives,
And so be bright-adorned beloved of the gods of the earth and heavens.

The Song of Orpheus

The Muses forever mark the fair song
Of a gentle child nursed within the valley of Helion
A poet born, the clear-eyed child of Apollon,
Much-lauded god whom the dark-tressed Muses love.
You who were nursed by them upon the golden drops of honey
To find its sweet favor for your singing tongue,
And the echoes of their whispered lullabies
Flowing like a caught breeze within your soul
Turning about, that shaking wind,
Twisting within the hollows carved from its fluid spin
Until upon the gust from your lips, that bardic song,
It rings in pure melody and then is gone.
For even as the loud-speaking wind takes hold of the prophetess,
And she nods her head in acquiescence, to be swept away
Upon the shuddering currents within her mind's quietness
The word of the god delivered in metered eloquence
From the soft part of her holy lips,
So too are you swept away, like a flower
Upon a swift-footed river, to be delivered where it may.
For the space of a breath you are not the flesh and blood,
The wearied flesh, but the immortal song
Its wind is yours escaping from your chest
And the mortal heart clenches in fearful protest
That the gusty breath once delivered past the tongue
Would forever to your memory be undone.
Never to be recaptured once gone,
That brief kiss of the god's immortal song,
Thou mantic, captured within the grasp of divine breath,
Forever esteemed, poet Orpheus.

About the Author

Lykeia is a priestess of Apollon, and a devotee of Artemis who attributes her poetic, written and artistic inspiration to the leader of the Muses. Other than inspiration, she has had the advantage of a BA in history with a minor in English Literature. She has happily had the opportunity to visit Greece and spend some time in Delphi, Olympia, Mykenae, Epidaurus and Athens. She is currently a resident of Anchorage, Alaska and is involved in several online Hellenic communities such as Hellenion and Neokoroi.

Illustrations

All illustrations in this book are either public domain or have been released into the creative commons by the photographers listed below.

Ludovisi Ares, Artemis Manicalunga, Poseidon Enthroned, The Departure of Apollo and Artemis, Hermes and the Goat Sacrifice, Hermes Ingenui, Silver Tetradrachm, Persephone and Hades, Dionysos Python in the Louvre, Young Dionysos, Silver Helios Coin of Rhodes by Marie-Lan Nguyen

Hephaestus and Thetis, Hera in the Staatliche, Athena in the Louvre, Eleusinian Hydria, Nereids and Triton, Calyx-Krater of Dionysos and Ariadne in Louvre by Bibi Saint-Pol

Artemis of Thrace by QuartierLatin

Bust of Hera by Romerin

Athena Holding Spear, Lekythos of Hermes by David Liam Moran

Apollon Greek Plate by Orlovic

Apollo in the NY Carlsberg by Chris O

Locri Pinax of Persephone and Hades by AlMare

Dionysos Mosaic by Vissarion

Daphne by Jakob Auer by Giulio Dottorpeni

Aphrodite and Adonis by Jastrow